BEYOND THE COBBLESTONES IN DUBLIN

An insider's guide to the best places to eat, drink and explore

FIONA HILLIARD

EXPLORE

BEYOND THE COBBLESTONES IN DUBLIN

CONTENTS

WELCOME TO DUBLIN

Dublin is a small city with a warm heart – and enough culture and craic to fuel a weekend stay or short break. Best of all, if you're based in the city centre, most of the action is within walking distance.

There is, however, a lot to be gained by going beyond the cobblestones. This guide introduces you to the city centre's most popular sights and attractions, but also challenges you to experience the places that shape modern Dublin – the cafes, bars, and restaurants loved by locals and the vibrant neighbourhoods that celebrate old traditions and new additions.

Living in Dublin, it's sometimes easy to take the city for granted – the closeness and convenience of the coastline, the top-tier pubs, and the abundance of interesting cultural attractions, many of which are free to visit. Writing this book, I've had to look at Dublin through a different lens. It has made me appreciate even more the things that make the Irish capital unique – and why it's so important for visitors to look beyond the obvious.

To help you get your bearings in Dublin, I've mapped out routes for you to explore the city in a way that makes the journey just as interesting as the main attractions. I've also included an overview of each of the areas featured in the guide – there's no wrong or right place to start your adventure, whether you head to the coast or straight to Temple Bar.

Enjoy exploring Dublin beyond the cobblestones.

Fiona

ABOUT DUBLIN

Dating back to 841, the city of Dublin owes its origins to the life-giving properties of a black pool – or 'dubh linn' if you know your cúpla focail (bit of Irish).

Sadly, for the Vikings who founded Dublin, the black pool in question wasn't a babbling brook of dark velvety stout (that came later), but rather the meeting point of two rivers, the Poddle and the Liffey. The two rivers formed a port (where Dublin Castle stands today), and this port became an important harbour for Viking boats, which developed into a thriving settlement.

THE LIFFEY: DUBLIN'S BUOYANT BOUNDARY
Today the River Liffey cuts cleanly through the centre of modern Dublin, dividing the city into a northside and a southside. Streets, villages, and suburbs on each side are identifiable by a postcode (even numbers for the southside, odd numbers for the northside).

COASTAL KALEIDOSCOPE
Stretching from Howth Head on the northside to Dalkey on the southside, prawn-shaped Dublin Bay serves up a juicy cocktail of coastal villages, islands, and beaches. Hop on the DART and head south for glimpses of the candy-striped Poolbeg Chimneys and sweeping Sandymount Strand, and discover seaside towns and villages like Monkstown, Dún Laoghaire, Sandycove, and Dalkey. Or journey northside and stop off in Malahide to explore its medieval castle and beautiful gardens, or Howth where spectacular hiking trails and some of Ireland's best seafood awaits.

WILD AND GREEN
Dublin's parks and green spaces are the gifts that keep on giving. Throughout the year they moonlight as markets, open-air galleries, and concert venues. In the summer months, fallow deer fawn can be found wandering amongst the woodland of Phoenix Park while the lakes of St Stephen's Green provide an urban habitat for mallard ducks and swans.

ABOUT DUBLIN

GET YOUR BEARINGS

Dublin's compact size makes it the ideal destination for a weekend stay or short break. And to ensure you make the most of your time, this guide zeros in on the essentials – the best places to grab a coffee or a bite to eat, the pubs loved by locals, plus the daytrips, cultural sights and attractions that will live on in your memory long after you've shared your escapades on social media.

A NOTE ON THE LISTINGS THROUGHOUT THIS BOOK

In the interest of helping you, the reader, navigate your way through the many wonderful places listed throughout this guide, the listings within each section run first in order of postcode, then alphabetically within each area. So the cafes in the Brews and Bakes chapter, for instance, in Dublin 1 appear first, in alphabetical order, followed by Dublin 2, etc. Then North County Dublin (Howth and Malahide, for example) follow the last Dublin postcoded neighbourhood, followed by South County Dublin (including areas such as Monkstown, Sandycove and Glasthule, and Dún Laoghaire).

A NOTE ON PRICING

Throughout this guide, you'll find a key to pricing under establishments that serve food. Here is a guideline on what each number of euro symbols means, but please be aware prices can always change so check ahead to ensure a place meets your expectations and suits your budget.

€ – average prices

€€ – above average prices

€€€ – pricey, but exceptional experience

DUBLIN

Key

1. Howth Harbour
2. Martello Tower Sandycove
3. Trinity College Dublin
4. Temple Bar
5. Christ Church Cathedral
6. Guinness Storehouse
7. Croke Park

NEIGHBOURHOOD INDEX

NEIGHBOURHOOD INDEX

Neighbourhood Index

NOTABLE NEIGHBOURHOODS

Although Dublin 2 is probably considered the most central area – and a good base – the city centre is compact and flat, which means you can easily get from A to B by foot. Meanwhile, the coastal villages and suburbs are just a short Luas, DART, or bus journey away. To help you make up your mind about where to start your adventure, here is a short introduction to each of the areas that appear in this guide. Dublin postcodes are easy to navigate – even numbers are on the southside of the Liffey, odd numbers are on the northside.

THE DOCKLANDS

The epicentre of Dublin's tech scene, the docklands or 'Silicon Docks' stretches from the International Financial Services Centre (IFSC) to Grand Canal Dock and pockets of Dublin 4 and covers both sides of the Liffey. Explore the story of Irish emigration at EPIC Museum, sip cocktails on the roof of Anantara The Marker Dublin Hotel, or give SUP a go at Surfdock.

DUBLIN 1

Thanks to The Spire, or The Spire of Dublin as it's officially known, there's no need to break out your map app – a 120 metre high stainless-steel pin has been conveniently dropped on Dublin 1. Market stalls meet Michelin stars in this area that has undergone an exciting regeneration in recent times. Leading the charge is Capel Street, a partially pedestrianised zone feted for its cafes, ethnic restaurants, Victorian bars, and LGBTQIA+ scene. Fine dining at Chapter One, cutting-edge fashion at Clerys, and some of the city's most underrated and thought-provoking cultural attractions can also be found in this neighbourhood, including the Hugh Lane Gallery, the Abbey Theatre, and 14 Henrietta Street.

NOTABLE NEIGHBOURHOODS

DUBLIN 2

From Dublin 1, cross the Ha'penny Bridge into Dublin 2. This is the Dublin you recognise from postcards and popular culture – the well-trodden cobblestones of Trinity College and Temple Bar, the majestic Georgian townhouses, the old-style pubs beloved by literary legends, and the much-photographed Molly Malone statue. But it's also home to the city's best shopping experiences – high-end retail on Grafton Street and homegrown fashion labels and independent boutiques around Drury Street and South William Street.

DUBLIN 6

A 25 minute walk, or short Luas ride or taxi journey from the city centre, the leafy suburbs of Ranelagh and Rathmines provide more than just a change of scenery – these Dublin 6 neighbourhoods boast serious brunch spots, cosy date-night restaurants, and bougie concept stores.

DUBLIN 7

Bordering Dublin 1, and to the north-west of the city centre, you'll find Dublin's creative heartland, aka Dublin 7. While you're in the neighbourhood, you can breakfast in a buzzy Stoneybatter or Phibsborough cafe, or check out locally made textiles and ceramics in Arran Street East. But whatever you do, make sure to drop into The Cobblestone in Smithfield for a traditional Irish music session. Hup.

DUBLIN 8

To the west of Dublin 2, you'll encounter some of the capital's oldest neighbourhoods – the Liberties, Portobello, and Kilmainham. The city's most visited attraction can also be found here – the Guinness Storehouse, as well as the Irish Museum of Modern Art (IMMA), and Kilmainham Gaol. The history of the Liberties goes back 800 years – the name was given to 'free' jurisdictions that existed outside of the city walls of Viking and Medieval Dublin. To this day, there is still a strong village-within-a-city vibe on Meath Street, Thomas Street and Francis Street, where a vibrant mix of markets, antique shops, bars and restaurants attract both locals and tourists. Meanwhile, Portobello has long been a melting pot of cultures. Once known as 'Little Jerusalem', in the 19th century, it was home to Dublin's Jewish community. That heritage lives on in Bretzel Bakery on Lennox Street. Amid the tangle of attractive Victorian redbrick houses, you'll also encounter artisan shops like Lennox Street Grocer and charming neighbourhood cafe Brindle Coffee & Wine.

NORTH OF THE LIFFEY

North of Dublin 1 and Dublin 7 and just 3km from Dublin city centre is Dublin 3, where its showpiece, Croke Park, dominates the Drumcondra skyline. Nearby in Glasnevin, Dublin 9, you can while away an afternoon discovering native and exotic plants in the National Botanic Gardens, pull up a stool in John Kavanagh – The Gravediggers pub and hear about its history and fabled clientele, or take a tour of the neighbouring Glasnevin Cemetery, where you can trace your ancestry and learn about Irish cultural and political icons.

NORTH COAST

On Dublin's north coast, the seaside villages of Howth and Malahide offer spectacular panoramic views of Dublin Bay, beaches, hiking trails, historic castles, and excellent seafood restaurants. All just a 25 minute DART journey from the city centre.

SOUTH COAST

Jump on the DART to the south coast, and discover the gourmet delights of Blackrock, Monkstown, Sandycove and Glasthule, the bustling harbour town of Dún Laoghaire (pronounced Dun Leary), and Ireland's 'Amalfi Coast'. Encompassing the heritage town of Dalkey and nearby Killiney, these scenic suburbs are famous for their sea-swimming spots, des res properties, and A-lister residents.

LITERARY DUBLIN

FULL-DAY ITINERARY

This full-day itinerary will take you south of the River Liffey by foot exploring the literary gems within Dublin 2.

8.30AM Start your day with breakfast at ① **Bewley's** on Grafton Street (see p. 53). The building itself – with a stained-glass window by acclaimed Irish artist Harry Clarke, cosy upholstered banquettes, open fireplaces, and an original Art Deco mosaic tiled facade – is something to marvel.

9.45AM Stroll down Grafton Street, taking in the lively atmosphere of buskers and flower sellers, and head straight towards the entrance of ② **Trinity College Dublin**. Pass through the front gates and take a walk around the cobbled campus, following the footsteps of famous alumni including Oscar Wilde, Jonathan Swift, Samuel Beckett, and more recently Sally Rooney, plus her star-crossed protagonists Connell and Marianne.

10AM Take a right on the Front Square and then a left towards the Old Library building (pre-booked tickets are necessary for entry). Inside, discover the precious ③ **Book of Kells**, a 9th-century manuscript that features intricate illustrations and Latin text (see p. 128). In the same building, you'll also find the spectacular Long Room. Regarded as one of the world's most beautiful libraries, the 18th-century building houses more than 200,000 of Trinity College's oldest books.

12PM Exit the Trinity College campus via the Arts Building and continue right onto Nassau Street. Cross the street and take a left onto Dawson Street. Stop by ④ **Hodges Figgis**, Ireland's oldest bookshop (see p. 193) – it's been in business since 1768 – and pick up a literary memento.

Across the street, you'll see ⑤ **St Ann's Church**, one of just six Dublin churches surviving from the 18th century, which is famous for its wood carvings and unique 'bread shelf' tradition. Since 1723, loaves of bread have been placed on a shelf by the altar, free to take for those in need. This is also where *Dracula* author Bram Stoker married Florence Balcombe in 1878.

1PM Take a right onto Duke Street and swing by one of James Joyce's favourite pubs, ⑥ **Davy Byrnes**, for lunch. If you're fully embracing the literary experience, make like Leopold Bloom in *Ulysses* and opt for a gorgonzola sandwich with a glass of Burgundy – it's still on the menu.

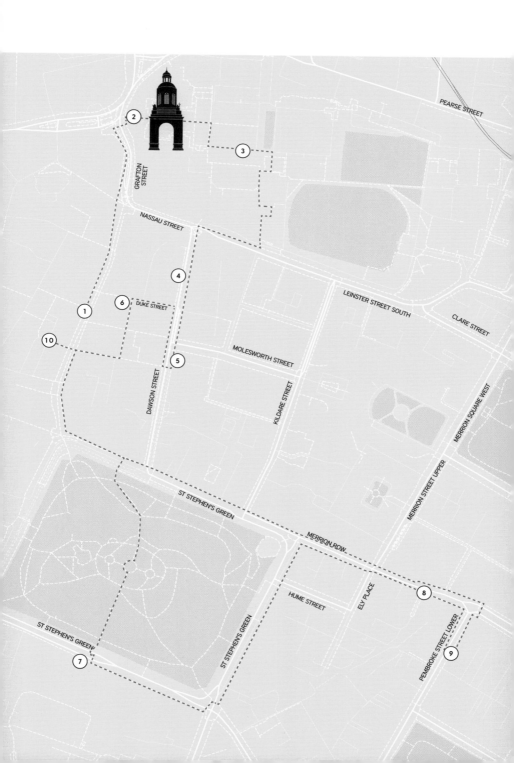

3PM Head towards the south side of St Stephen's Green Park to ⑦ **Museum of Literature Ireland (MoLI)** (see p. 129). The museum celebrates Ireland's literary heritage and the Irish tradition of storytelling through immersive exhibitions. There's also the opportunity to view rare literary editions from the National Library of Ireland, including a prized 'Copy No. 1' of *Ulysses*.

5.30PM Walk back towards Grafton Street, and take a right, strolling in the direction of Merrion Row and Baggot Street. Drop into ⑧ **Toners** pub (see p. 110) for a well-earned pint – back in the day, the bar was a favourite haunt of W.B. Yeats – before heading towards Pembroke Street.

8PM Named after a character from *Knocknagow*, an Irish bestselling novel from the 19th century by Charles Kickham, ⑨ **Matt the Thresher** is an opulent gastropub specialising in fresh, wild Irish seafood, classic fish and chips, and Irish dry-aged steaks – just the place to chat about the day's events over dinner.

10PM Stay on for drinks or jump in a taxi to ⑩ **McDaid's** on Harry Street (see p. 100), a favourite haunt of Brendan Behan's, and where James Joyce set the opening of his short story 'Grace'.

THE LIBERTIES
FULL-DAY ITINERARY

Filled with history, creativity, personality … and the faint smell of roasted hops and barley – 'eau de Guinness' – the Liberties is one of Dublin's most vibrant quarters. This full-day tour should give you an insight into the neighbourhood's oldest, boldest, and most interesting attractions.

10AM Kick things off at ① **The Fumbally** and order the Fumbally Eggs – a spicy, cheesy, eggy mishmash served on toasted sourdough brioche. This breakfast and lunch spot prides itself on its great coffee and local ingredients, but the calm home-from-home atmosphere is what makes it a great place to start your day.

11AM After breakfast, head north towards Patrick Street and onto St Patrick's Close, where you'll find ② **Marsh's Library**. Dating back to 1707, it was the first public library in Ireland. Much of the original interior is preserved, including beautiful dark oak bookcases and 'cages' where readers were once imprisoned with books to prevent them from stealing rare titles. As you might expect, Marsh's Library has some pretty impressive literary links – James Joyce mentions the library in *Ulysses*, Bram Stoker visited several times while researching *Dracula*, and Jonathan Swift was a governor of the library.

12PM Continue north towards Patrick Street and ③ **Christ Church Cathedral**. Founded in 1030 on the site of a Viking church, the cathedral sits in the former heart of Medieval Dublin. Inside, there are curiosities at every turn, including the tomb of Norman knight Strongbow, the heart of St Laurence O'Toole, a rare copy of the Magna Carta, and even a mummified cat and rat. It's also possible to climb to the belfry, but be prepared – it's a narrow, twisty, 86-step hike.

1PM From Patrick Street, head west towards Francis Street and ④ **Two Pups Coffee** (see p. 63). The industrial-chic cafe is not only popular with locals, but also their four-legged friends … well, the clue is in the name. Order one of the chunky batch-bread toasties or try one of the colourful salads. And leave room for dessert – the cakes at the counter are far too good to resist.

2PM From here, continue north up Francis Street, where a slew of antique shops including ⑤ **Anonymous** and ⑥ **Yeats Country Antiques** will tempt you with mid-century furniture and Victorian knick-knacks, or west towards Meath Street, where you'll discover vintage treasures of another kind – local street traders who will be only too happy to offer you a bargain and a taste of Dublin wit. All roads lead to Thomas Street.

4PM At Thomas Street, make your way towards the ⑦ **National College of Art and Design (NCAD)**. College alumni include fashion designer Orla Kiely, W.B. Yeats, and milliner to the stars Philip Treacy. The college's gallery is open to the public and hosts exhibits throughout the year – check the website for details about events taking place during your visit.

4.45PM Continue along Thomas Street, then turn left onto Crane Street. At the end of Crane Street, turn onto Market Street. You should see the ⑧ **Guinness Storehouse** – a temple to Ireland's most famous export – on your right (see p. 137). Once the fermentation plant of the Guinness brewery, the Storehouse is laid out to allow you to explore the ingredients, culture, and history that shaped the company. Don't miss the marketing exhibition that features some of the brand's most famous advertising campaigns. The pièce de résistance, though, is a pint in Gravity Bar, where you can enjoy spectacular 360-degree views over the city, including the Wicklow Mountains, Phoenix Park, Dublin Bay, and even Howth.

7.45PM From Crane Street, head back east on Thomas Street. Book well in advance to secure a table at ⑨ **Variety Jones** (see p. 83). The Michelin-starred restaurant is headed up by chef Keelan Higgs and offers a short, inventive menu that's perfect for sharing – most of the dishes are cooked on or beside an open wood fire, while the wine list is considered and available by the glass.

10PM Move on to ⑩ **Vicar Street** and catch a late-night gig or duck into ⑪ **John's Bar & Haberdashery** next door for a nightcap before taking a cab back to your base.

HOWTH

FULL-DAY ITINERARY

This coastal excursion will take you on a scenic tour of Howth, a pretty fishing village located 18km north-east of Dublin city.

9AM Make your way to Pearse Station and take the DART northbound to Howth station. In just 35 minutes, you'll be swapping city sights for sea air, rugged landscapes, and some of Ireland's best seafood.

9.45AM Pop in to ①**Póg** (meaning 'kiss' in Irish) on Harbour Road to fuel up on a breakfast of fried eggs, black pudding and bacon, smashed avocado toast, or a syrupy stack of pancakes (see p. 64).

10.30AM Coffee in hand from ②**Bodega** (just outside Howth Market, see p. 43), take a walk along the ③**East Pier** until you reach the lighthouse – you might even spot the wild seals surfacing alongside the harbour for scraps from the local fishing boats. If you're visiting on Saturday, Sunday or a Bank Holiday Monday, Howth Market is worth browsing with its mix of street food, artisan crafts, jewellery, and natural cosmetics.

11AM For a more challenging ramble, tackle the 6km ④**Cliff Path Loop**, a gentle two-hour hike that begins next to the DART station. Expect green and wild landscapes blanketed in yellow furze and magenta heathers, as well as views of Lambay Island and Ireland's Eye. The trail also passes Balscadden Bay, a turquoise stretch of water popular with sea swimmers.

1PM Having worked up an appetite, head to ⑤**Mamó** for lunch – booking advised (see p. 85). The sustainable, seasonal menu makes the most of local ingredients such as Howth honey, salad leaves and vegetables from McNally Family Farm in North Dublin, and fresh lobster that land daily on the pier. Alternatively, weather permitting, get in line at ⑥**Beshoff Bros** and enjoy a fish and chips feast by the harbour.

3PM Stroll through Main Street – ⑦**Surround** (see p. 204) is a great place to pick up a gift or memento – before popping into ⑧**OMG** ice-cream parlour on Abbey Street for a classic 99 cone or a towering, TikTok-worthy tub of soft serve with all the bells and whistles.

HOWTH

3.45PM Walk back to (9) **Howth Harbour** to board an (10) **Island Ferries** cruise from the West Pier (pre-booking required online). The 45 minute tour takes you on an adventure around Ireland's Eye, where you can catch a close-up look at the local seals and puffins. If you're visiting between April and September, there's also the option to disembark and spend time exploring the island.

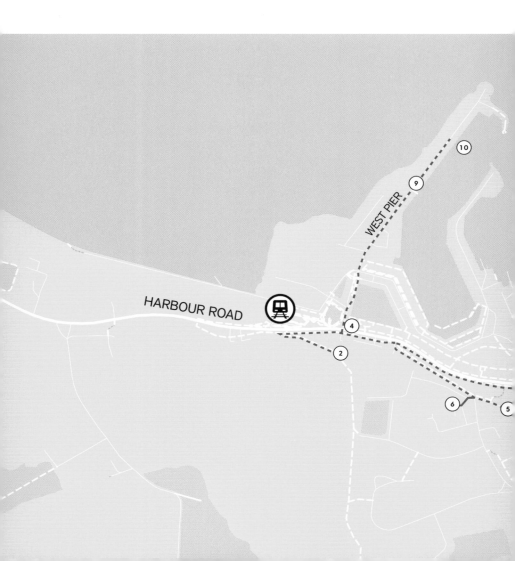

4.30PM Call into 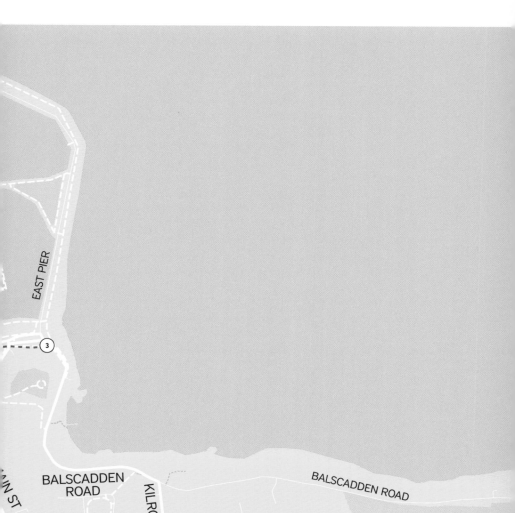⑪ **The Abbey Tavern** (see p. 116) for a cosy fireside pint.

6.30PM Take the DART from Howth Station back to Dublin city centre, alighting at Pearse Station.

EAST PIER

③

BALSCADDEN ROAD

KILROCK RD

N ST

BALSCADDEN ROAD

SOUTH COAST

FULL-DAY ITINERARY

This seaside adventure will take you on a whistle-stop tour of some of the most scenic towns and villages on Dublin's south coast.

9 AM From Nassau Street, take the number 7A bus, alighting at Monkstown.

9.40AM For a proper, 'set-you-up-for-the-day' breakfast, pay a visit to (1) **Salt** in Monkstown village. Managed by the Avoca crew, the cafe's feel-good morning menu includes big comforting bowls of creamy organic porridge, a signature full Irish (organic eggs, bacon, sausage, local black pudding and portobello mushrooms), and sweet, crunchy, yoghurt-smothered granola.

11AM Afterwards, browse the neighbouring row of gift shops and boutiques including (2) **Seagreen** (see p. 205) and (3) **The Blue Door** – from candles and jewellery to woollen blankets and scarves, there's plenty to choose from if you're looking for something Irish and stylish to take home. Next, follow the coast road towards Dún Laoghaire (pronounced Dun Leary), spot yachts in the marina, join the local dog walkers and joggers for a bracing walk along the East Pier, or head straight to (4) **Teddy's Ice-Cream** and order one of its famous 99 cones. Within a short stroll, the (5) **People's Park** provides the perfect oasis. If it's Sunday, check out the park's weekly market (see p. 180), where you'll find great coffee, ethnic food stalls, art, crafts, and local produce.

12PM From Dún Laoghaire, continue towards Sandycove and its landmark (6) **Martello Tower**. Now a free museum dedicated to writer James Joyce (closed Mondays), it features a re-creation of Joyce's living quarters – he spent six nights in the tower in 1904 and the experience proved so profound that he chose it as the location for the opening scene of *Ulysses*. There's also a roof terrace where you can enjoy uninterrupted views of Dublin Bay. Just a stone's throw away is the (7) **Forty Foot**, which has been attracting Dublin's sea swimmers for over 250 years – if you're planning to take a dip, pack your swimming togs and towel (dryrobe if you're fancy).

1PM For lunch to go, drop into (8) **Cavistons** deli in nearby Glasthule (see p. 87) and pick up some gourmet snacks, or if it's Sunday, call into (9) **The Butler's Pantry** in Sandycove for your bougie takeaway. In Sandycove, turn left at Harbour Road, where you'll encounter Bullock Harbour, a stop-you-in-your-tracks view of Howth on the far side of the bay,

and maybe even some friendly seals. Walking uphill towards Dalkey, take a left at Coliemore Road, where the road is flanked by some of Ireland's most beautiful (and most expensive) properties. As the road sweeps downhill towards Coliemore Harbour, you'll catch a glimpse of Dalkey Island. Continue uphill towards Vico Road and turn left at ⑩ **Dillon's Park** (see p. 162). Take a seat at one of the tables, set out your picnic, and drink in the spectacular scenery.

2.30PM Continuing uphill from here, you'll pass yet more A-list residences in Killiney – the neighbourhood that Bono, Enya, and The Edge call home. It's also where you'll find Vico Baths, the popular local swimming spot that was a hit with Hollywood actor Matt Damon during his extended lockdown stay in Dalkey in 2020.

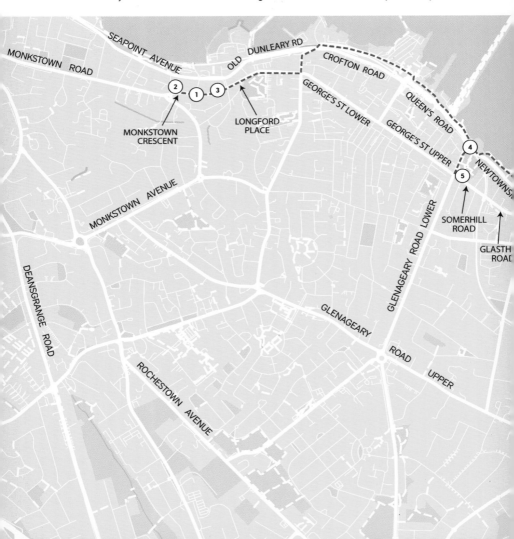

3PM Following the road downhill, you'll reach Dalkey village. Pop into the excellent ⑪ **The Gutter Bookshop**, warm yourself by the stove, and browse the shelves for something by the local talent (Maeve Binchy and George Bernard Shaw were both Dalkey residents), or a Joycean novel, or have a chat with the staff, who'll be happy to recommend something, then make your way to ⑫ **Dalkey Castle** (book online for a guided tour) before heading next door for a pint in ⑬ **The Queens**.

6PM Take the DART from Dalkey Station back into Dublin city centre, alighting at Pearse Station.

BREWS AND BAKES

Dublin was traditionally known for being a city of tea lovers, but over the past decade or so, a new brew has stolen our hearts – speciality coffee. So much so that there are now 181 coffee shops for every 100,000 people in the capital.

Some that started out as independent cafes and street carts now have multiple locations across the city, including Colin Harmon's 3fe (see p. 32) and Karl Purdy's Coffeeangel (see p. 36), while others like The Little Cactus in Stoneybatter (see p. 39) march to their own unique beat. Then there are the counter treats: the flaky croissants and sticky cinnamon buns – Camerino (see p. 33) and Proper Order (see p. 38) are renowned for their solid selections. And all is not lost for tea aficionados – Clement & Pekoe (pictured opposite, also see p. 34) on South William Street serves some of the finest blends in Dublin.

This chapter reveals the best of the best places to find a good brew – and something sweet to pair it with – in the city.

3fe

Try Dublin's most famous speciality coffee in its flagship Grand Canal Street cafe.

32–34 Grand Canal Street Lower, Grand Canal Dock, Dublin 2

Bus: 77A, C1, C2, C4
DART: Grand Canal Dock

EUR
€

W
3fe.com

Swapping investment banking for coffee beans, Colin Harmon founded 3fe (third floor espresso) in 2009 and now operates multiple cafes around Dublin as well as a roastery that supplies many of the city's best-loved cafes. Sustainability is key for Harmon. Coffee is purchased from farmers using a direct-trade model, and the cafes keep waste to a minimum by composting grounds.

Popular with local tech company employees, as well as anyone who enjoys good coffee, 3fe's Grand Canal Street cafe also serves breakfast and brunch favourites such as pancakes, avocado toast, and granola, as well as a generous selection of cakes, scones and pastries – the almond croissant is my pick of the bunch.

Camerino

Basement cafe with top-notch cakes.

37 Merrion Square East,
Dublin 2

Bus: 4, 7, 7A, 15A, 26
Luas: Green Line, Dawson or
St Stephen's Green

EUR
€

W
camerino.ie

In the basement of the Goethe-Institut Irland building, Canadian expat Caryna Camerino has created the perfect cafe space, whether you're sitting down for lunch – the sandwiches are legendary – or whiling away an hour or so with a Roasted Brown coffee or Clement & Pekoe tea. Of course, then there are the cakes, pastries and cookies. Camerino prides itself on its freshly baked selection – all tantalisingly displayed on the counter. Choose from wholesome scones, sweet little gingerbread men, giant cookies, tray bake slices, and whimsically decorated cupcakes – depending on the time of year, there are always new seasonally-inspired creations to discover.

Brews and Bakes

Clement & Pekoe

An elegant tea and coffee house on South William Street.

---

50 South William Street,
Dublin 2

Bus: 13, 14, 15, 16, 46A
Luas: Green Line,
St Stephen's Green

EUR
€

W
clementandpekoe.com

With its elegant black interiors, Art Deco chandeliers, and meticulously arranged tea caddies, there's a real sense of grandeur about South William Street's Clement & Pekoe.

The coffee selection changes regularly and is sourced from international roasteries, as well as the Dublin-based Imbibe, Upside, and Groundstate, while the high-grade loose-leaf tea selection includes black teas, matcha, white teas, oolong, Pu-erh, and fruit teas. Recently, Clement & Pekoe has also launched its own brand of craft kombucha, which is brewed in its Blessington Street HQ. Order to go and grab a seat on the bench outside or relax and enjoy the tearoom's decadent surroundings.

Cocobrew

Serving speciality coffee in Temple Bar since 2015.

5 Bedford Row, Dublin 2

Bus: 16, 27, 39, 39A, 46A, 77A, C4

Luas: Green Line, Westmoreland

EUR

€

W

cocobrew.ie

If you've attended festivals or events in Ireland, you might recognise the Cocobrew brand from its distinctive VW Kombi. Founded by Tony Devito in 2015, Cocobrew is a cafe and roastery in Temple Bar that specialises in Brazilian, Nicaraguan, and Colombian beans. Plant-based cakes, cookies and treats are provided by Dublin-based Sweet Almond bakery, while a talented and enthusiastic in-house team deliver friendly service and skilful latte art. Interiors-wise, Cocobrew is rustic and welcoming. You can either sit in at one of the custom-made 'coffee tables' – actual coffee beans are encased within the glass – or perch on the window seat outside and absorb the colourful sights and sounds of Temple Bar.

Brews and Bakes

Coffeeangel

Speciality coffee to go.

One of Dublin's OG specialist coffee shops, Coffeeangel was founded by Karl Purdy in 2003 and has grown from a mobile street cart to a handful of locations around Dublin city including its compact Leinster Street cafe, which is just steps away from the National Gallery of Ireland. This is a great spot to grab a quality takeaway coffee if you're shopping or exploring the Trinity College/Nassau Street/Merrion Square area. Indoor and outdoor seating is also available if you've got time for a sit-down and there's also a nice selection of baked goods and artisan pastries in the form of sausage rolls, croissants and scones.

15 Leinster Street South,
Dublin 2

Bus: 7A, 11, 15A, 16, 46A, 83
Luas: Green Line, Dawson

EUR
€

W
coffeeangel.com

Kaph

*The cool kid of
Drury Street.*

---

31 Drury Street, Dublin 2

 /

Bus: 14, 15, 16, 77A, 83
Luas: Green Line, Trinity

EUR
€

W
kaph.ie

Opened in 2013 by Chris Keegan, Kaph has been the cool kid of Drury Street for some time now. Personally, I love what it brings to the street – not only excellent coffee (Kaph serves 3fe using 18/19mg per shot, meaning you're getting a lot of bang for your buck), but also its pavement bench, which sits outside the front window. Literally part of the furniture of Drury Street, it's a great spot to hang out with a takeaway coffee, tea or matcha and watch the comings and goings of this creative neighbourhood.

For a rainy-day pick-me-up, grab a cosy table inside or upstairs and one of Kaph's delicious baked treats.

Proper Order

Creative Smithfield cafe founded by champion baristas.

7 Haymarket, Smithfield, Dublin 7

Luas: Red Line, Smithfield

EUR

€

W

properordercoffeeco.com

Located close to the Old Jameson Distillery, Proper Order is a popular Smithfield coffee spot run by champion baristas Niall and Aliona Wynn. Inside, serious-looking laboratory-style equipment gives way to a short and sweet menu that features a constantly rotating range of coffee beans from some of Europe's leading roasters as well as creative, seasonal latte options.

Whitewashed walls and subway tiles create a bright and clean aesthetic, while stools, wooden counters, and minimalist tables and chairs provide no-nonsense seating arrangements.

Stoneybatter's No Messin' bakery delivers the sugar highs in the form of square doughnuts, 'hun buns', and other assorted delights.

The Little Cactus

*Coffee, cactus plants,
and vintage clothing
in Stoneybatter.*

1a Prussia Street, Dublin 7

Bus: 39, 39A, 46A, 70

EUR

€

W

thelittlecactus.ie

Taking inspiration from the concept cafes they had encountered on their travels in Vancouver, Dubliners Jamie and Kate decided it was time Dublin got a piece of the action. And no better place to open their coffee/vintage/plant shop than in the creative heartland of Stoneybatter. Located on Prussia Street, The Little Cactus serves speciality coffee from Bailies Coffee in Belfast, matcha, herbal teas, and hot chocolate, as well as eggs and avocado toast – with bread from Bretzel Bakery, vegan-friendly cakes, and pastries. Bright white walls, cacti, and leafy plants create an earthy, 'urban Eden' vibe, and there are rails of vintage clothing to browse while you wait for your brew.

Two Boys Brew

Brewing up a storm in Phibsborough since 2016.

The boys in question are Kevin and Taurean. The brew is Root & Branch Coffee Roasters. And they've been making magic in Phibsborough since 2016. The decor is very much clean lines and industrial chic – minimalist wooden Scandi-style tables and seating. Dangling house plants add vibrant pops of green, while a small number of outdoor tables accommodate local puppies and their parents. Service is super-warm and friendly. If you're ordering your coffee to go, it's reassuring to know that the cups are 100 per cent compostable. If that's not an incentive to make a return visit, the twice-baked almond croissant certainly is – in fact, the entire baked goods selection is top notch.

375 North Circular Road, Phibsborough, Dublin 7

Bus: 4, 38A, 46A, 83, 122, 155

EUR

€

W

twoboysbrew.ie

Brindle Coffee & Wine

Late-opening Portobello cafe with wine, coffee, and its own playlist.

34 Lennox Street, Dublin 8

Bus: 15, 16, 46A, 83

EUR

€

W

brindlecoffeewine.com

If Richard Curtis ever decides to shoot a blockbuster in Dublin, this Portobello cafe has romantic comedy written all over it. It's got amazing coffee – courtesy of Wicklow-based roastery Roasted Brown. It's got wine – organic and interesting low-intervention types. It's got four-legged creatures – all sorts of pooches are welcome ... cats too. It has outside seating – in the form of some very Instagram-worthy deckchairs. And it opens late – until 8pm on weekdays and Sundays and until 9pm on Fridays and Saturdays. They've even got the soundtrack sorted. Brindle's 'mixtape' is the cafe's home tasting kit that includes eight curated organic wine samples plus a fun accompanying playlist of songs.

Legit

Legitimately good coffee in a former butcher's shop.

1 Meath Mart, Meath Street, Dublin 8

Bus: 13, 27, 123, G1, G2

EUR

€

W

legitcoffeeco.com

Located on Meath Street, in the heart of the Liberties, Legit was founded in 2015 by Damien and Jay, a Frenchman and a Brazilian, who transformed a former butcher's shop into a warm and inviting cafe that has become as famous for its freshly baked cakes, sausage rolls, sandwiches and pastries as it is for its superb coffee. The coffee, by the way, is Brazilian origin, sourced from local Irish roasteries, including Full Circle. Well-placed plug sockets and floor-to-ceiling windows also make Legit a lovely place to work for an hour or two.

If you're browsing the nearby Liberty Market between Halloween and Christmas, pop in and try Legit's seasonal lattes – gingerbread, salted caramel, and pumpkin spice.

Bodega

*Coastal caffeinator
in Howth.*

Conveniently located close to Howth Market, Bodega has been caffeinating locals, hikers, and daytrippers since 2017. Founded by Jack Rickard, who was inspired by the coffee scene in New York and Melbourne, Bodega's pared-back black exterior and bare lightbulbs give it a cosy shipping-container vibe. Coffee comes from Full Circle Roasters, a sustainable roastery based in Dublin. Staff are skilled, efficient and friendly and power through weekend queues with a smile. Seating-wise, there are bar stools indoors, and wooden benches, tables, and seating surrounding the entrance. When it comes to sweet treats, there's a good selection of artisan creations, including gluten-free and vegan-friendly options. It's also worth noting that Bodega is ready and waiting to provide your fix seven days a week, even when the market is closed.

Unit 1, Howth Market, Howth

Bus: 6, H3
DART: Howth Station

EUR
€

W
bodega.ie

Hatch

*A cosy Melbourne-inspired cafe
in Glasthule village.*

Founder Mealla Tarrant hatched the idea to launch a speciality coffee shop in Dublin while watching an espresso being expertly pulled by a barista in Melbourne's tiny Brother Baba Budan cafe. In 2016, she realised her dream by opening Hatch in Glasthule village. Still going strong – with long queues to prove it – Hatch is compact in size, with exposed bricks and a small seating area to the left of the fireplace adding character and cosiness inside. Outside, there are tables and stools designed for outdoor chats, along with thoughtful dog bowls for four-legged friends. The coffee comes from 3fe's Dublin roastery and takeaway cups are 100 per cent compostable. For an extra sugar hit, choose from cakes, cookies and pastries – the rockstar of the bunch is the award-winning Hatch Swirl.

♀	🚌 / 🚆	**EUR**
4 Glasthule Road,	Bus: 7, 7A	€
Sandycove	DART: Sandycove and	
	Glasthule	

BRUNCH AND BREAKFAST

Having the time to enjoy a leisurely breakfast or brunch is one of the joys of travel. Fortunately, in Dublin there are ample places that encourage you to do just that.

Soak up the Art Nouveau splendour of Bewley's (see p. 53), enjoy a boozy brunch in Dillinger's in Ranelagh (see p. 57), or make like Anthony Bourdain and embrace the breakfast of champions in Slattery's (see p. 51). For something uniquely Irish, try the boxty-based dishes at Gallagher's Boxty House (see p. 54), or the big, hefty batch loaf sandwiches at Farmer Browns (see p. 58). For something a little different, sample Argentinian flavours at Alma (see p. 62), the Dublin 8 cafe famous for its aesthetically pleasing brunch creations.

Whether your perfect morning in Dublin looks like an all-out greasy full Irish, smashed avocado on sourdough, syrupy pancakes, eggs to go, or a fried chicken wing and cocktail feast, the following pages will help you plan the most important meal of the day.

Brother Hubbard

A warm welcome, contemporary flavours, and outdoor seating await on Capel Street.

153 Capel Street, Dublin 1

Bus: 39, 70, 83, 145
Luas: Red Line, Jervis

EUR

€

W

brotherhubbard.ie

They say a recession is a great time to start a business. Proof of the pudding is Brother Hubbard, the Capel Street cafe founded by Garrett Fitzgerald and James Boland in the depths of Ireland's economic downturn in 2012.

It is now a highly successful chain, with offshoots in Portobello, Ranelagh, and Arnotts (Liffey Street entrance), but the original Brother Hubbard on Capel Street is the one to beat for atmosphere and coveted outdoor seating.

On the brunch menu, if available the Moroccan eggs zaalouk is always a good call. So too is 'the basic', Brother Hubbard's delicious interpretation of a full Irish – toasted homemade sourdough, two eggs, grilled bacon, and roasted tomato sauce. The coffee is from Farmhand Coffee, Brother Hubbard's sibling business. It's roasted on Capel Street and is excellent.

Slattery's

A Capel Street early house with a world-famous full Irish breakfast.

---

129 Capel Street, Dublin 1

Bus: 39, 70, 83, 145
Luas: Red Line, Jervis

EUR

€

W

slatterys.bar

Chef and author Anthony Bourdain certainly boosted Slattery's international profile when he tucked into a full Irish breakfast here in 2006 (they still have the newspaper cuttings to prove it), but this Capel Street boozer has been indulging early-rising Dubliners since 1892, when the then Victorian Gin Palace acquired a 7am opening licence to accommodate traders from the newly opened Dublin Corporation Markets on Mary's Lane.

So, what can you expect from the Bourdain-approved brekkie? It's a gut-busting full Irish – McCarron's rashers, award-winning Tournafulla sausages, black and white pudding, tomato, hash brown, fried egg, toast, and a choice of tea or coffee. Pint optional.

Brunch and Breakfast

The Woollen Mills

A lively weekend brunch spot with a roof terrace.

42 Ormond Quay Lower, Dublin 1

Bus: 26, 37, 39, 39A, 70, 83, 83A, 145, 151, C4, G2
Luas: Red Line, Jervis; Green Line, O'Connell – GPO

EUR
€

W
thewoollenmills.com

In a past life, The Woollen Mills was a haberdashery and drapery shop that once employed James Joyce. These days, it's a popular industrial-chic-style eatery with a loyal weekend brunch following.

Inside, it's all about the funky factory feel – whitewashed walls, vibrant orange chairs, and subway tiles. Outside, there's a heated terrace that's close enough to eavesdrop 'the Hags with the Bags' – the two bronze ladies resting with their shopping bags. The covered roof terrace, meanwhile, is a cosy space with fairy lights and Liffey views – and even lovelier on a sunny Saturday or Sunday, when brunch is served. Speaking of brunch, the menu is extensive. Go all out with eggs, waffles, and bacon, or mix and match a couple of the starters – the signature 'woolley wings' are always good. When it comes to cocktails, the selection is sweet, spicy, and fun – case in point, the habanero pineapple margarita – tequila, Cointreau, pineapple, lime, and habanero chilli. Even on the greyest of days, it's like sunshine distilled.

Bewley's

Brightening up mornings
on Grafton Street
since 1927.

_____

📍

78–79 Grafton Street, Dublin 2

🚌/🚏

Bus: 27, 39, 39A, 70, 155
Luas: Green Line,
St Stephen's Green

EUR
€

W
bewleys.com

Bewley's, the grand old dame of Grafton Street, is renowned for its glazed sticky buns, pots of tea, and Art Nouveau stained-glass windows designed by Irish artist Harry Clarke. Back in the day, breakfast at Bewley's meant the standard full Irish breakfast of eggs, sausage, rashers, and pudding. Recently, though, they've branched out into brunch territory, with an altogether more cosmopolitan offering of dishes like overnight oats, avocado burgers, and smoked salmon and eggs flatbread. There's also a revamped full Irish served with Bewley's stout and treacle brown soda bread and a choice of 'heritage buns' – cinnamon, cherry, or almond – the type of treat your nanna would have looked forward to after a day of shopping in town.

Brunch and Breakfast

Gallagher's Boxty House

Try boxty – a traditional Irish potato bread – in Temple Bar.

20–21 Temple Bar, Dublin 2

Bus: 16, 27, 39, 39A, 46A, 77A, 155, C4

EUR
€

W
boxtyhouse.ie

'Boxty on the griddle, boxty on the pan, if you can't make boxty, sure you'll never get a man.'
Some of the best food in the world has humble origins, and boxty is no different. It gets its name from the Irish 'arán bocht tí' meaning 'poorhouse bread'. A cross between a potato cake and a flatbread, boxty is thought to have originated in the border counties – Leitrim, Cavan, and Fermanagh – and was traditionally eaten at Halloween. The key ingredients are potatoes, flour, milk and butter. Not only has Gallagher's Boxty House in Temple Bar perfected the technique of making boxty, but they've elevated boxty to new flavour heights. Brunch is a boxty extravaganza – boxty finds its way into boxty dumplings, boxty pancakes, boxty bread, and even boxty crisps. As this tends to be a popular spot for tourists, reservations are advised.

Herbstreet

Sustainable brunch classics with waterside views.

9 Hanover Quay, Docklands, Dublin 2

Bus: 60, 77A, 151, C1, C2, C3, G1

EUR

€

W

herbstreet.ie

When it comes to brunch in the docklands, Herbstreet's waterfront location makes it a bit of a weekend hot spot. Once smugly seated, you can peruse the brilliantly balanced menu: there's the sweet stuff – mounds of buttermilk pancakes and French toast, the healthy option – a super salad studded with goji berries and bee pollen, and the deliciously dirty – spicy buffalo wings with Cashel Blue dip and a turkey burger with smoked bacon and cranberry relish. And it wouldn't be brunch without eggs. Herbstreet has the classics covered – Benedict, Florentine, and royale, accompanied by the homemade cheesy English muffin. Leave room for dessert – the baked New York-style cheesecake is always incredible. Brunch is served from Friday to Sunday; booking is advised.

Brunch and Breakfast

Keoghs

The early bird catches breakfast at Keoghs.

1–2 Trinity Street, Dublin 2

Bus: 26, 77A
Luas: Green Line, Trinity

EUR
€

W
keoghscafe.ie

Open from 6.45am Monday–Saturday and 8.30am on Sundays, Keoghs cafe has been greeting early birds with its welcoming glow for over 30 years. Bursting with seasonal fruit, and smothered in butter, its warm handmade scones are definitely worth waking for, while the fried breakfast takes you on a little culinary adventure around Ireland – free range eggs, West Cork black and white pudding, Galway sausage, and plum tomatoes, served with sourdough toast. Creamy porridge, stunning omelettes and virtuous vegetarian and vegan options ensure everyone gets off to the right start. The cafe's outdoor seating on Trinity Street is another major plus.

Dillinger's

Mediterranean small plates and mezcal cocktails in Ranelagh.

47 Ranelagh, Dublin 6

Bus: 11, 18
Luas: Green Line, Ranelagh

EUR
€€

W
dillingers.ie

Dillinger's has been delighting weekend brunch parties in Ranelagh since 2009 when John Farrell and Leo Molloy opened their casual American-diner-style restaurant. A recent revamp has seen the brunch menu break away from its previous shtick, swapping out spicy wings, fried chicken, and BBQ ribs for a rich medley of Irish seafood, Spanish tapas, and Latin-American and Mediterranean flavours. Alongside classic cocktails and spirits, they're mad about mezcal, with no less than five agave-based creations to choose from on the menu. The margaritas are some of the finest you'll find in Dublin, and there's also a solid wine and beer selection.

Farmer Browns

Burgers and brunch with an American twang.

---

170 Rathmines Road Lower, Dublin 6

Bus: 15, 18, 83

EUR

€

W

farmerbrowns.ie

Sisters Grace and Finnuala opened their Rathmines branch of Farmer Browns on St Patrick's Day 2016, just in time for the restaurant's loyal brunch fans to enjoy its sunny, pooch-friendly outdoor terrace. If you've never tried their brunch menu, you're in for a treat. It's a flavour fest of US-sized proportions – and portions – juicy 4oz beef burgers, club sandwiches on thick Bretzel Bakery batch bread, tempura cauliflower wings, cheesy nachos and all-American fried chicken and waffles. Superfood salads and vegan options also pack a punch. Cocktails are decent – and some are available by carafe. There's also a serious selection of Irish craft beers.

Mad Yolks

A cracking good breakfast spot in Smithfield.

Unit 4, Block C, Smithfield Square, Dublin 7

Bus: 37, 39, 39A, 60, 145, C4
Luas: Red Line, Smithfield

EUR
€

W
madyolks.ie

Brothers Hugh and Eoin O'Reilly founded Mad Yolks in 2018. Graduating from a food truck to a full-on bricks-and-mortar restaurant, Mad Yolks totally goes to town with its egg-and-brioche-based all-day breakfasts. The 'bad yolk' – toasted brioche filled with two free range fried eggs, smashed black pudding, streaky bacon, beef tomato, applewood cheddar, rocket, and tangy tomato relish – is a tasty revelation, while the famous 'mad yolk' – a spicy, cheesy, scrambled creation – is a delicious cure-all wrapped up in a brioche bun. Click-and-collect ordering means you can enjoy your eggs on the go if you're that way inclined. Otherwise, there's indoor and outdoor seating and a chill, sunny vibe.

Slice

A tiny, award-winning Stoneybatter cafe with big brunch energy.

56 Manor Place, Stoneybatter, Dublin 7

Bus: 37, 39, 39A, 70

EUR

€

W

asliceofcake.ie

You'll find Slice just off the main street in Stoneybatter. It's very much a tiny but mighty situation. The small, light-filled space offers an epic brunch selection, oven fresh cakes and pastries, cold-pressed juices, and quality coffee from 3fe. On weekends, brunch is served all day. The buttermilk pancakes loaded with poached fruit, ricotta, and caramel are outrageously good, while the herby, zingy, Naniji's achaar provides the loveliest wake-up call for your tastebuds – spicy McNally organic beetroot achaar pickle, labneh, sourdough, poached eggs, seeds, and heirloom tomatoes. When it's sunny in the 'batter, Slice's outdoor terrace to the front is the place to be – four-legged friends are welcome too.

31 Lennox

A friendly neighbourhood brunch spot in Portobello.

31 Lennox Street, Dublin 8

Bus: 15, 16, 46A, 83

EUR
€

W
31lennox.ie

George Bernard Shaw once said, 'There is no sincerer love than the love of food.' Not far from his Portobello birthplace is 31 Lennox Street, a friendly redbrick neighbourhood restaurant with a buzz so casual it makes you feel like you're calling around to a friend's house for brunch. That is, if your friend has an outrageous talent for crispy chicken wings. Or smoky bacon Benedict. 31 Lennox's brunch menu gives the people what they want – there's Italian-inspired dishes like lamb polpette and Caprese salad, plus a hearty full Irish served with rosemary potatoes, vegan-approved mushrooms on sourdough, and buttermilk pancakes with peach mascarpone. They've got cocktails too ... and outdoor tables – everything you need to start your weekend in style.

Brunch and Breakfast

Alma

Bringing the soul of Argentina to the South Circular Road.

12 South Circular Road, Dublin 8

Bus: 16, 68, 122

EUR
€

W
alma.ie

Meaning 'soul' in Spanish, and spelling out the first initials of the four Argentinian sisters that run the cafe, Alma serves up one of the most Instagrammable brunches in Dublin. The menu is a tasty tango of seasonal Irish produce and Argentinian flavours. Alma's poached eggs – free range poached eggs on sourdough with smashed avocado, garlic portobello mushrooms, feta cheese, and salsa criolla (a colourful salsa of bell peppers, tomatoes, onion, olive oil, and vinegar) is a real showstopper. Dulce de leche pancakes – buttermilk pancakes with moreish dulce de leche (a sweet and sticky condensed milk-based, caramel-coloured spread), seasonal fruits, and brandy and orange mascarpone are something special. Coffee is from Two Fifty Square, which is roasted in Rathmines. As the space is quite small – and popular on weekends – my advice is to book in advance.

Two Pups Coffee

Pooch-friendly feasts and first-rate coffee on Francis Street.

74 Francis Street, Dublin 8

Bus: 27, 49, 77A

EUR
€

W
twopupscoffee.com

Francis Street's origins can be traced back to 1233, when a Franciscan friary was established on a site close to St Patrick's Street. Perhaps a nod to the patron saint of animals, it's only fitting that some 800 years later Two Pups Coffee made its home on this street. The dog-friendly cafe is all about good vibes, seasonal, fresh, and creative food, plus great coffee. Decor-wise, there's a minimalist feel, with white walls softened by cosy fairy lights and leafy house plants. Out front, there's a lovely outdoor terrace for al fresco brunching. Hungry? Order the beetroot Turkish eggs, and you can't go wrong – it's a flavour bomb of spiced beetroot yoghurt, fried free range eggs, McNally organic balsamic and caraway roast beets, crumbled feta, candy pickled beetroot, paprika butter, cashews, and herbs. Delish.

Póg

A love letter to pancakes in Howth.

Harbour Road, Howth

Bus: 6, H3
DART: Howth Station

EUR
€

W
ifancyapog.ie

In Madrid, they say 'el beso'; in Florence, they say 'il bacio', and in Dublin, we say 'póg'. Named after the Irish word for kiss, this sweet little chain of cafes has been on the go since 2014. Its Howth cafe on Harbour Road is one of the most recent additions to the family. Avo toast on Bretzel sourdough, wholesome acai bowls, and spicy nduja eggs are something to write home about, but the dedicated pancake menu is a real love letter. Signature protein pancakes get a flavour boost from your choice of berries, biscuit, chocolate drops, granola, plus gooey Nutella, caramel, or good-old-fashioned maple syrup – vegan and gluten-free options are also available. When it comes to drinks, there's a choice of fresh juices, smoothies, matcha, iced teas, herbal teas, regular tea, and excellent coffee.

Bibi's

Healthy choices and sea air in Dún Laoghaire.

---

2 Windsor Terrace,
Dún Laoghaire

Bus: 7, 7A, 45A, 59
DART: Sandycove and Glasthule

EUR
€

W
bibis.ie

Portobello brunch favourite Bibi's opened a sister cafe close to the Dún Laoghaire seafront in 2021, much to the delight of Forty Foot regulars. Sea-green walls and industrial-style lamps create a rustic angler's nook vibe that immediately draws you in. For spectacular sea views, pull up one of the stools by the window or grab one of the few tables outside and check out Howth across the bay. The brunch menu is all about healthy, seasonal choices – it changes regularly, but if squash eggs (poached eggs with butternut squash, garlic yoghurt, coriander, and chilli butter) are on offer, get your order in quick – it's always a great shout.

DINNER AND DRINKS

With Dublin's reputation for world-class ingredients and exceptional hospitality, visitors can look forward to incredible dining experiences in beautiful and eclectic surroundings. In fact, thanks to the current crop of casual and fine dining restaurants, there's never been a better time to eat out in Ireland's capital.

All across the city, skilled and talented chefs are pushing the boundaries to deliver imaginative menus that make the most of the finest Irish produce.

If you're only in Dublin for a short amount of time, it's worth knowing the lay of the land – where to find the culinary masterpieces, standout vegan and vegetarian dishes, and buzzy hot spots.

From Michelin fine dining at Chapter One (see p. 70) and Variety Jones (pictured opposite, also see p. 83) to suburban neighbourhood favourites like Host (see p. 80), Big Mike's (see p. 86), and Nightmarket (see p. 81), not to mention gastropubs, seafood restaurants and ethnic eateries, this chapter has all the inspiration you need to plan a night on the town.

Chapter One

Michelin star fine dining on Parnell Square.

18–19 Parnell Square, Dublin 1

Bus: 46A, 122, 155
Luas: Green Line, O'Connell Upper or Parnell

EUR
€€€

W
chapteronerestaurant.com

With its history of Michelin stars, Chapter One has long been one of Dublin's most revered restaurants. And its relaunch in 2021 as Chapter One by Mickael Viljanen has seen the restaurant enter a new era of excellence.

Located on Parnell Square in the basement of a Georgian house that whiskey distiller John Jameson once called home, Chapter One's interior is a celebration of Irish art, design, and craft set against a backdrop of rustic granite walls. This feeling of luxury refinement very much sets the tone for Mickael's intricate menu and curated dining experiences. The Chef's Table allows guests to get up close and personal with the Chapter One kitchen and enjoy a tasting menu immersed in culinary theatre. Meanwhile, the Midleton Room and Demi-Salle provide intimate private dining spaces for small groups. An extensive wine list showcases artisan producers as well as well-established domaines.

Terra Madre

One of Dublin's best kept secrets for authentic Italian cuisine.

13a Bachelors Walk, Dublin 1

Bus: 7A, 26, 39, 46A, 70, 145, 151, C1
Luas: Red Line, Jervis; Green Line, O'Connell – GPO

EUR
€€

W
terramadre.ie

Venturing down the steps to the small, basement-level Terra Madre restaurant on Bachelors Walk feels like you're entering a secret portal into Tuscany. Inside, it's a casual, rustic space and just like its 'mother earth' name suggests, the menu of this Italian-run spot is wholesome, sustainable, and seasonal. Expect rich flavours and regional Italian favourites such as pappardelle ragout, carpaccio, and tagliolini alla gricia, and a short but sweet wine list. In keeping with the 'home from home' vibe, service is friendly and informal, while the restaurant has room for only around 18 diners, plus a tiny outdoor terrace, so booking is advised.

The Winding Stair

A bookshop and restaurant with inspiring views.

---

40 Ormond Quay Lower (near Liffey Street Lower), Dublin 1

Bus: 26, 37, 39, 39A, 70, 83, 83A, 145, 151, C4, G2
Luas: Red Line, Jervis;
Green Line, O'Connell – GPO

EUR
€€

W
winding-stair.com

Taking its name from a collection of poems by William Butler Yeats, The Winding Stair is one of Dublin's oldest and best-loved independent bookshops. Climb the winding staircase and you enter an elegant restaurant of the same name, where the focus is on classic Irish flavours with matched wines, beers and ales. And then there is the view – it feels like an extra little privilege if you get a table by the window. Overlooking the Liffey and the iconic Ha'penny Bridge, the windows offer a unique vantage point that perfectly captures Dublin's energy, especially after dark when neon signs glow from Merchants' Arch and lights dance on the river below.

Delahunt

Modern Irish cuisine and a cosy cocktail bar.

39 Camden Street Lower,
Dublin 2

Bus: 9, 14, 15A, 16, 83, 122
Luas: Green Line,
St Stephen's Green

EUR
€€

W
delahunt.ie

Back in Victorian times, Delahunt was known to Camden Street locals as a greengrocer. Selling everything from teas to turkeys, the shop was even mentioned in James Joyce's *Ulysses*. These days, Delahunt Restaurant and Bar is an elegant and refined space with polished wood floors, marble-top tables, leather banquettes, and discreet mahogany snugs.

Lunch and evening menus emphasise seasonal Irish ingredients, while the innovative vegan and vegetarian menus deliver vibrant, flavourful plates.

Upstairs, The Sitting Room cocktail bar brings opulent mid-century vibes with low-slung furniture, original fireplaces, and a bay window overlooking Camden Street. This cosy den is one of Dublin's best kept secrets for pre-dinner drinks or a candlelit nightcap.

Etto

Big flavours on small plates.

18 Merrion Row, Dublin 2

Bus: 38A, 39, 39A, 70, 155
Luas: Green Line, Dawson

EUR
€€

W
etto.ie

Proving that good things really do come in small packages, Etto – meaning 'small' or 'cosy' in Italian – is a casual blink-and-you'll-miss-it wine bar and restaurant on Merrion Row.

The menu is as sleek and streamlined as the restaurant's minimalist decor, championing seasonal ingredients and an interesting mix of Irish and Mediterranean flavours. Meanwhile, the wine list is extensive and focuses on small independent producers.

Whether you go for options like the classic côte de boeuf, or the tasty vegan-friendly roast potato gnocchi, be sure to leave room for dessert – the red wine prunes and vanilla mascarpone is ridiculously good.

Limited seating means the restaurant fills up pretty quickly, so advanced booking is advised.

Hang Dai

Sample Sichuan, Cantonese, and Mandarin dishes in a buzzy Blade Runner-style setting.

20 Camden Street Lower, Dublin 2

Bus: 9, 14, 15A, 16, 83, 122
Luas: Green Line,
St Stephen's Green

EUR
€€

W
hangdaichinese.com

Camden Street's Hang Dai restaurant may be decked out with a dancefloor, disco ball, and booths within a subway carriage, but it's the food that really shines.

Roast duck and dumplings are specialities, and there's a vibrant selection of snacks and starters on the menu, including Connemara oysters, crispy squid, and cheeseburger spring rolls. The restaurant's custom-built, wood-fired oven adds extra theatre to locally sourced char siu pork and applewood-fired Skeaghanore duck mains. Meanwhile, an inspired vegetarian menu means everyone is invited to the party.

Upstairs, the Gold Bar spins tunes late into the night as mixologists craft unique takes on classic cocktails.

Dinner and Drinks

Las Tapas de Lola

A ray of Spanish sunshine on Wexford Street.

---

12 Wexford Street, Dublin 2

Bus: 14, 15, 15B, 16, 83
Luas: Green Line, Harcourt

EUR
€€

W
lastapasdelola.com

Let Barcelona-born Anna Cabrera and Dubliner Vanessa Murphy take you on a tour of Catalonia, Galicia, and Jerez through an extensive menu of sharing platters and small plates at their stylish tapas restaurant on Wexford Street. A friendly, casual atmosphere makes this spot just the ticket for catch-ups with friends, date nights, or after-work gatherings. Kick off with one of Las Tapas de Lola's signature cocktails or an aperitivo – tinto de verano, a mix of Spanish red wine and fizzy lemon, is a revelation. This sweet and refreshing alternative to traditional sangria is perfect for summer evenings on the terrace. For a dessert to remember, close out with churros con chocolate – a rich, delicious version of the classic Spanish féria snack.

The Garden Room at The Merrion

An elegant restaurant within The Merrion, offering al fresco dining in summer.

The Merrion Hotel, Upper Merrion Street, Dublin 2

Bus: 15A, 15B, 38, 38A, 39A, 44, 70, 155
Luas: Green Line, Dawson

EUR
€€

W
thegardenroom.ie

Executive head chef Ed Cooney and his team at The Garden Room at The Merrion deliver a relaxed dining experience in five-star surroundings.

From rockstars to presidents, The Merrion is the hotel of choice for VIP visitors to the Irish capital. But The Garden Room shakes off any potential for pretension, classing itself as 'a less formal affair by a formal garden'. Floor-to-ceiling windows overlooking the manicured gardens give the space a light, airy feel, and on warmer summer days, tables spill out onto the terrace, transforming the private courtyard garden into one of the city's most sought-after venues for al fresco dining.

The menu is robust and celebrates locally sourced produce – expect riffs on Irish venison, seafood, and dry-aged steaks and creative and considered vegan options.

Zaytoon

A Camden Street institution serving halal-friendly, flavour-packed fast food.

44–45 Camden Street Lower, Dublin 2

Bus: 9, 14, 15A, 16, 83, 122
Luas: Green Line,
St Stephen's Green

EUR
€

W
zaytoon.ie

Iranian owners Jamshid Kamvar and Azad Shirazi launched Camden Street's Zaytoon in 2005 with the goal of elevating the humble kebab from greasy post-pub snack to an authentic, fresh, and flavourful dish that could be enjoyed not just as a late-night feed, but also as a tasty lunch or casual dinner option. They've taken a back-to-basics approach, sourcing their fish, halal meat and poultry from Irish suppliers, charcoal grilling their kebabs, and adding fresh herbs and Persian spices to deliver a true Iranian experience. Vegan and vegetarian options mean there's something to keep everyone happy. Recently renovated, the Camden Street restaurant is open weekdays from lunchtime to midnight and from midday to 4.30am on weekends. Prepare for early morning queues – a kebab or shish meal from Zaytoon is part and parcel of a great night out in town.

The Old Spot

A Michelin-approved gastropub serving up a legendary Sunday roast.

14 Bath Avenue, Sandymount, Dublin 4

Bus: 4, 7A, C1, C2
DART: Grand Canal Dock

EUR
€€

W
theoldspot.ie

Sandymount's The Old Spot is nothing if not consistently good. It's a sentiment echoed by folks at Michelin who have featured The Old Spot in its *Eating Out in Pubs* guide for the past four years.

Classics like The Old Spot pie of the day and the beer-battered fish and chips are a hit with weekday crowds, while the big, hearty roasts are a sell-out on Sundays.

Comfy banquettes and a cosy, lived-in decor give the pub a warm, inviting feel. Between the lively atmosphere and the excellent food, you might easily be persuaded to stay put for an afternoon.

Host

A warm welcome and a feast of small plates awaits in Ranelagh.

----

13 Ranelagh, Dublin 6

Bus: 18, 44, 61
Luas: Green Line, Ranelagh

EUR
€€

W
hostrestaurant.ie

Host's premise of 'small plates, fresh pasta, quality cuts' translates to a slick, minimalist neighbourhood restaurant with a clever, concise menu. And like any good host, this Ranelagh spot makes a fantastic first impression.

The menu is designed to be a shared experience, and options change daily, based on seasonal ingredients. The simplicity is refreshing. There are three small plate options, three fresh pasta options, three options from the grill, and three side plate options. Alternatively, there is a chef's menu for two – perfect for date nights – that features a range of small plates and a dessert to share. Meanwhile, the wine list is equally meticulous, with a selection available by the glass.

Nightmarket

*Destination dining
and far-flung vibes
in Ranelagh.*

120 Ranelagh, Dublin 6

Bus: 11, 18, 44, 61
Luas: Green Line, Ranelagh

EUR
€€

W
nightmarket.ie

Ever since former KOH alumni Conor Sexton and Jutarat Suwankeeree brought their flavour train to Ranelagh in 2017, they've been pulling in the crowds. Inspired by the night markets of Chiang Mai and Hua Hin, Nightmarket serves up authentic Thai flavours in a cosy, intriguing restaurant setting that's designed to make you feel like you've been transported to a luxurious underground metro station. Steamed dumplings, pad thai, and fragrant curries are elevated to new heights, while an innovative drinks menu sees classic cocktails infused with Irish spirits. Asian beers and an extensive wine list complete the first-class dining experience.

Dinner and Drinks

L. Mulligan Grocer

A Stoneybatter gastropub where sustainable Irish ingredients and craft beers are the order of the day.

18 Stoneybatter, Dublin 7

Bus: 37, 39, 39A, 70
Luas: Red Line, Smithfield

EUR
€€

W
lmulligangrocer.com

Just a short stroll from the Jameson Distillery is L. Mulligan Grocer, a gastropub that once upon a time was a neighbourhood grocer.

If you're after a pint of the black stuff, you've come to the wrong pub. This is a Guinness-free zone. Instead, the bar is stocked with craft ales, lagers, and stouts. Menu-wise, there are gourmet versions of traditional bar snacks like Scotch eggs, and hefty mains such as fish and chips, collar of pork, black pudding burgers, and vegan/vegetarian-friendly creations including spiced cauliflower. All ingredients are sourced from local producers, chicken and pork are free range, and fish is sustainably sourced from independent fishing boats. Meanwhile, greens and vegetables are harvested from the owner's own allotment.

Variety Jones

Keelan Higgs's Michelin-starred restaurant serves up fiery delights in the heart of the Liberties.

78 Thomas Street, Dublin 8

Bus: 13, 123

EUR
€€€

W
varietyjones.ie

Enigmatic from the get-go – there's zero signage on the outside – Variety Jones is one of the capital's boldest and most exciting restaurants. Bookended by a cafe and a vintage store at 78 Thomas Street, the interiors are minimalist and industrial, with exposed brickwork, pipework, and concrete floors. And the elemental theme doesn't end there. Head chef Keelan Higgs, along with his brother Aaron, have embraced natural wines and a custom-built, wood-burning hearth, with embers from oak and birch logs providing a unique flavour bed for the short, imaginative menu. Advance booking is advised for this award-winning hot spot.

Shouk

A taste of the Middle East on the northside.

---

40 Drumcondra Road Lower,
Drumcondra, Dublin 9

Bus: 1, 13, 16, 41
Train: Drumcondra

EUR

€

W

shouk.ie

Headed up by Israeli-born chef Alon Salman, Shouk reminds me just how much I love Middle Eastern food. Inside, there's a cosy, relaxed set-up, but on a sunny day the outdoor terrace is something special. Shouk's menu prioritises vegetarian dishes – Jaffa salad, Moroccan aubergine, and beetroot bowls inject colour and zing, while special mention goes to the whole roasted head of cauliflower covered in tahini and jewel-like pomegranate seeds – a real crowd-pleaser. Freshly baked pitas stuffed with brisket, lamb or chicken certainly make for generous, meaty mains. There are Spanish and Belgian beers on tap, a sweet and spicy cocktail selection, and a well-priced wine list. For BYOB, there's a €10 corkage fee.

Mamó

A harbour-facing Howth bistro that celebrates local seafood and sustainable produce.

Harbour House, Harbour Road, Howth

Bus: 6, H3
DART: Howth Station

EUR
€€

W
mamorestaurant.ie

Dream team Killian Durkin (formerly Chapter One) and Jess D'Arcy (ex-Etto front of house) bring their wealth of experience to this tiny but mighty seafront gem to deliver contemporary dining in a relaxed, friendly setting.

The seasonal menu features organic greens and veg from McNally Family Farm, lobster sourced fresh from Ireland's Eye, while Higgins Butchers in Sutton provides the fundamentals for the côte de boeuf. The signature dish – cod chip, a Jenga-style creation of fried confit potato topped with a taramasalata frosting – is a real standout.

Grab an outdoor table for lunch if the sun is shining.

Dinner and Drinks

Big Mike's

Destination surf 'n' turf restaurant.

Upper Rock Hill, Blackrock

Bus: 4, 7, 7A
DART: Blackrock

EUR

€€–€€€

W

michaels.ie/big-mikes

Situated in the seaside suburb of Blackrock, Big Mike's is big on flavours, big on choice, and big on atmosphere. Owner Gareth (Gaz) Smith has created a destination restaurant with chef Peter Byrne serving up fresh local seafood, responsibly sourced meats, and good times. Seafood and shellfish is very much the star of the show – Dublin Bay prawns, clams, mussels, crab claws, and lobster are sourced daily. Dry-aged steaks and pan-fried monkfish are other specialities, and there's a well-crafted wine list. This is a hugely popular spot so advance booking is advised. Walk-ins are welcome in the cocktail bar for drinks and bar snacks.

Cavistons

Seafood, sea views, and old-fashioned charm in Glasthule.

56 Glasthule Road, Sandycove

Bus: 7, 7A, 59
DART: Sandycove and Glasthule

EUR
€€

W
cavistons.com

Cavistons has been part of Glasthule's history and fabric for over 60 years and is renowned for its Bloomsday celebrations every 16 June, when it hosts a Leopold Bloom-themed street party complete with period costumes and traditional breakfast – read pork kidneys and assorted offal.

Having started out as a fish shop, the family-run business now encompasses a gourmet food hall and a recently renovated restaurant. Carrying on Cavistons' tradition of serving quality seafood, the new space has elevated the experience with the addition of a wine and cocktail bar with stunning views of Dublin Bay and art courtesy of the neighbouring Wilton Gallery.

SNACK ATTACK

Everyone in Dublin has their favourite takeaway snacks that are a weekend treat, late-night feast, or hangover cure. Comforting reliables, they deliver joy and sustenance in equal measure. For your convenience, I've recommended the best places in the city to try them out.

SPICE BAGS

Unique to Dublin, the spice bag is thought to have originated in The Sunflower Chinese in Templeogue in 2010. Although variations do exist, the key ingredients are chips, crispy chicken strips/chicken balls, chillies, red and green peppers, and onions. The steamy ingredients are thrown together with spices in a brown paper bag to be enjoyed as a greasy mishmash. Xi'an Street Food (28 South Anne Street) does a decent version of the original. Token (72–74 Queen Street, Smithfield) has a vegan version, while Bites by Kwanghi (83 Sir John Rogerson's Quay) puts an interesting spin on things with its Spice Bag Bao dish. Duck Hong Kong BBQ (15 Fade Street) goes one step further with its Duck Spice Bag – chips, crispy duck, sliced onion and peppers flavoured with Duck's special spice mix.

PIZZA BY THE SLICE

DiFontaine's (22 Parliament Street) landed in Dublin in 2002. The late-night pizza joint was founded by returned expats who wanted to bring the New York 'slice' experience to Dublin. Thanks to DiFontaine's, you can drop in, grab a slice of freshly baked New York-style pizza, then go about your night. Just a stone's throw from P. Mac's pub, Bambino (37 Stephen Street) is another late-nighter, serving NYC and Sicilian-style 'grandma' (focaccia-based pizza) slices to go.

MAGICAL KEBABS

Dublin's love affair with kebabs started in 1982 when the first Abrakebabra (66 Dame Street and 11 Rathgar Road, Rathmines) opened in Rathmines and introduced the donor kebab to late-night crowds. Some Dubliners can't get enough of its magic. Actor Colin Farrell is said to have been awarded a gold card for his well-publicised loyalty to the fast-food restaurant's kebab and chips.

In the noughties, Iranian duo Jamshid Kamvar and Azad Shirazi brought their signature charcoal-grilled, Persian-style kebabs to the masses with the opening of Zaytoon (14–15 Parliament Street and 44–45 Lower Camden Street), and they've been a hit with hungry night owls ever since.

'CHIPPER' CHIPS

The best chips in Dublin are soft, squidgy, and piping hot. They're shovelled into a white paper bag that overflows into a larger brown paper bag. Then they're doused in copious amounts of vinegar and lashings of salt. You'll find 'proper' chips like these in old-style Italian-owned chippers such as Morelli's (134 Thomas Street) or from the crème de la crème – Dublin's oldest chipper, Leo Burdock (2 Werburgh Street, Christchurch, and 4 Crown Alley, Temple Bar), which has been serving fish and chips from its flagship location on Werburgh Street since 1913.

CHICKEN FILLET ROLLS

Whether enjoyed as a hangover cure or a trusty lunchtime sandwich, the chicken fillet roll is another one of Dublin's culinary wonders. The most basic versions consist of a French baguette roll with mayonnaise or butter, breaded fillet of chicken – usually spicy or Southern-fried – shredded lettuce and cheese, but other fillings of your choice can also be added. Chicken fillet rolls can be found all over town in small convenience stores, newsagents, petrol stations or supermarkets with a deli counter – Centra in Stoneybatter (12 Stoneybatter, Dublin 7) does a particularly good one.

PUBS AND BARS

'Good puzzle would be cross Dublin without passing a pub.'
Not much has changed since 1904, when Leopold Bloom
uttered these words in James Joyce's Ulysses.

Pubs have always played an important role in Dublin's
culture. They are places where we go to meet friends and
socialise ... to celebrate and commiserate life's wins and
losses ... to watch sport, catch a gig, and have the craic.

From the pubs that pride themselves on their cosy
atmosphere and quality pints like Mulligan's (see p. 101) and
Kehoe's (see p. 99) to the ones that prioritise 'ceol agus craic'
(music and good times) like The Cobblestone (see p. 113) and
O'Donoghue's (see p. 102), this chapter features a selection of
the capital's most beautiful, interesting and historic, including
Victorian boozers beloved by writers – some of which have
changed little since Joyce's time – lively music venues, and
elegant and award-winning cocktail bars.

Pantibar

Cocktails, fun and frolics in Capel Street's bubbliest bar.

The home of 'The Queen of Ireland', Panti Bliss, Pantibar has been welcoming Dublin's LGBTQIA+ community since 2007. The Capel Street landmark's giant neon sign serves as a beacon for everything that's fun and fabulous about this northside neighbourhood.

7–8 Capel Street, Dublin 1

Bus: 39, 70, 83, 145
Luas: Red Line, Jervis

EUR
€

Drop into the bar during the day and enjoy pints of prosecco or Panti's Pale Ale in a chill atmosphere. After dark and on weekends, expect high drama in the form of lip sync extravaganzas, DJ sets, quizzes, bingo, and drag shows. Her majesty might even grace the stage.

During Pride weekend, Pantibar provides the backdrop for the parade's biggest after-party.

The Grand Social

Lively bar and gig space with a festival atmosphere.

35 Liffey Street Lower, Dublin 1

Bus: 37, 39, 39A, 46A
Luas: Green Line, O'Connell – GPO; Red Line, Jervis

EUR
€

W
thegrandsocial.ie

Just a short walk from Ha'penny Bridge, this lively bar, music venue and sometime flea market promises good times whether you are checking out one of its market events or catching an after-dark gig. It's a bit like a music festival with a roof – in fact, there's a retractable roof in the upstairs beer garden, so there's no danger of rain-soaked pints. And like any good festival, The Grand Social offers a solid line-up, from weekly quizzes to Afrobeats, indie and trad rock nights, plus an impressive selection of international beers. Upstairs, the rooftop beer garden serves cocktails and is a great place to catch live sports events on the big screen.

Pubs and Bars

Grogan's

A landmark Dublin 2 pub famous for its outdoor terrace and toasted sandwiches.

---

15 South William Street, Dublin 2

Bus: 7A, 13, 14, 15, 16, 39, 39A, 46A, 155
Luas: Green Line, St Stephen's Green

EUR
€

W
groganspub.ie

It may have first opened its doors in 1899, but this small but lively spot only really hit its stride in the 1970s, when barman Paddy O'Brien left another pub to join Grogan's. He took his best customers – writers, journalists and poets – with him, and it's fair to say that the pub's no-music, no-television policy did much to encourage conversation and banter among regulars and blow-ins. To this day, Grogan's (and its famous toasted sandwiches) still attracts a bohemian crowd, and its outdoor terrace provides a great spot from which to people-watch on South William Street and Castle Market.

Kehoe's

A Victorian watering hole with friendly crowds and some of the best pints in Dublin.

9 South Anne Street, Dublin 2

 /

Bus: 16, 39, 39A, 145, 155
Luas: Green Line, Dawson

EUR
€

W
kehoesdublin.ie

Kehoe's on South Anne Street calls itself a 'country pub in the heart of the city'. It's an accurate description of the Victorian bar, which still retains many original features, including stained glass and cosy snugs. Kehoe's was established in 1803 and made a name for itself as a literary hangout in the 1940s and '50s. These days, you'll find a steady mix of tourists and after-work crowds. On a sunny summer's evening, you'll be lucky to find elbow room on the street outside – but do persevere – you'll be rewarded with one of the best pints in Dublin.

McDaid's

A literary classic with a colourful past.

3 Harry Street, Dublin 2

Bus: 15, 16, 39, 39A, 70, 145, 155
Luas: Green Line,
St Stephen's Green

EUR
€

Located on Harry Street, McDaid's is a tall, narrow pub with an intriguing history. In the 18th century, the building housed the Dublin City Morgue, then later it became a chapel, which explains the high ceilings and Gothic-style windows. In its most recent incarnation as a pub, it was a favourite haunt of writers including Brendan Behan, Flann O'Brien, and Patrick Kavanagh. Good Guinness and conversation are still very much the order of the day. Seats are a rarity on weekends, when much of the crowd spills out onto the street, so drop in on a weekday afternoon if you want to experience the surroundings over a quiet pint.

Mulligan's

A timeless pub unspoiled by modern distractions.

8 Poolbeg Street, Dublin 2

Bus: 39A, 145, 155
Luas: Green Line, Trinity
DART: Tara Street

EUR
€

Mulligan's on Poolbeg Street has several claims to fame: It is one of Dublin's oldest pubs – established in 1782, originally situated on Thomas Street. It was also name-checked in James Joyce's short story 'Counterparts'. In the 20th century, Mulligan's was popular with actors from the nearby Theatre Royal and journalists from *The Irish Times* and neighbouring *The Irish Press* newspapers – it was even visited by a pre-presidential John F. Kennedy in the 1950s, while he was working as a journalist for Hearst newspapers. These days, a no-television policy ensures good banter, while a friendly and experienced bar crew guarantee perfectly crafted pints.

Pubs and Bars

O'Donoghue's

Beat a path to Merrion Row for music, craic, and a lively heated beer garden.

Renowned for being the birthplace of legendary Irish folk band The Dubliners, O'Donoghue's on Merrion Row is always buzzing with an even mix of locals and visitors. Drop in for traditional Irish music seven nights a week. Inside, the bar is something of a time capsule – expect original 1960s decor (including vintage upholstery and black and white photos).

On weeknights, the outdoor heated beer garden is a popular spot with after-work crowds. On weekends, you'll be lucky to find standing room, especially if there's a rugby match on in town.

15 Merrion Row, Dublin 2

Bus: 38A, 39, 39A, 70, 155
Luas: Green Line, Dawson

EUR
€

W
odonoghues.ie

P. Mac's

Craft beer, board games, and great tunes on Stephen Street.

28–30 Stephen Street Lower,
Dublin 2

Bus: 14, 15, 15B, 16, 140
Luas: Green Line,
St Stephen's Green

EUR
€

Located on Stephen Street, P. Mac's is one of my favourite Dublin pubs. It's a lovely, mostly candlelit space with cosy snugs, vintage French decor, board games including Monopoly, Connect 4, and Jenga, and arcade games. The craft beer selection is extensive and there's an excellent playlist of '90s and noughties indie, grunge, and rock music. One of its other unique selling points is its retro selection of Tayto-brand crisps – Chickatees, Wheelies, even Banshee Bones (all favourites from my Irish childhood) ... Sometimes it's the little things that really make a place.

Pubs and Bars

Peruke & Periwig

Music-themed cocktails in a former wigmaker's shop.

31 Dawson Street, Dublin 2

Bus: 4, 7, 7A, 39, 39A
Luas: Green Line, Dawson

EUR
€–€€

W
peruke.ie

Set in a three-storey Georgian townhouse on Dawson Street, Peruke & Periwig is a compact cocktail bar named after a popular style of 18th-century wigs. While it may sound eccentric on paper, the theme translates into some really fun and lavish Georgian-inspired decor – bookcases, velvet furnishings, a portrait gallery, clocks and various antiques.

I also love the music-themed cocktail menu – familiar favourites take on different genres; there's the Smells Like Teen Spirits (Appletini), Whiskey in the Jar (Old Fashioned), and Nothing Comparis to You (Negroni). The ground floor is usually standing room only, but upstairs there are two cosy, decadently decorated floors where you can linger over small plates and drinks.

The Auld Dubliner

A buzzy Temple Bar pub with live music 'til late.

24–25 Temple Bar, Dublin 2

Bus: 16, 37, 39, 39A, 46A, 70, 77A, 155, C4
Luas: Green Line, Westmoreland

EUR
€€

W
aulddubliner.ie

Chances are you'll hear The Auld Dubliner before you even reach its front door. This popular Temple Bar pub is a magnet for weekenders and stag and hen groups, largely because it pumps out live music for most of the day and night and doesn't take itself too seriously. There's usually a mix of lively, quality trad bands and seasoned guitar slingers belting out covers – requests are welcome. As it's a busy spot, seats are a rarity, especially after dark, but it's all part of the fun. Food-wise, its take on the traditional Dublin coddle (a salty stew of pork sausages, rashers, potatoes, carrots, and onion) is well worth a try if you can nab a table at lunchtime.

Pubs and Bars

The Long Hall

A Victoriana dream famous for its delicious pints and warm welcomes.

51 South Great George's Street, Dublin 2

Bus: 14, 15, 15A, 16, 83, 145

EUR

€

Red-and-white-striped canopies and swirly signage make quite the entrance, but it's the lovely atmosphere and even lovelier pints that really hit the spot. Licensed since 1766, The Long Hall on South Great George's Street is one of Dublin's oldest and best-loved pubs. The fact that the pub's decor has changed little since an 1881 makeover only adds to the appeal. Expect genuine Victorian fixtures and fittings, goldleaf embellishments, ruby-coloured walls, ceilings and carpets – plus, you might even spot The Boss, Bruce Springsteen, if he's playing in Dublin – it's one of his favourite hangouts when he's in town. He wouldn't be the first famous face to grace the pub. Brendan Behan was no stranger to a jar here, while some scenes from Phil Lynott's 'Old Town' music video were shot at the bar.

The Rooftop Bar at Anantara
The Marker Dublin Hotel

Enjoy cocktails on the roof and stunning views of the docklands.

Anantara The Marker Dublin
Hotel, Grand Canal Quay,
Docklands, Dublin 2

Bus: 47, 77A, C2
DART: Pearse Station

EUR
€€

W
anantara.com/the-marker-dublin

One of Dublin's most popular spots for summer sundowners, Anantara The Marker Dublin Hotel's rooftop bar and terrace offers 360-degree views over the city, taking in the Dublin Mountains and the Irish Sea.

The cocktail menu is a mix of classics, Marker staples, non-alcoholic options, and seasonal creations, including its signature cucumber and elderflower martini – a refreshing blend of gin, elderflower, cucumber and lime. A light, specially created rooftop menu by executive chef Gareth Mullins features delicious sharing plates inspired by land and sea.

Preference is given to hotel guests and the bar operates on a first come, first served basis. Morning rooftop yoga is also available over the summer months and is open to non-residents as well as hotel guests.

Pubs and Bars

The Stag's Head

A cinematic Victorian-era pub hosting regular events.

1 Dame Court, Dublin 2

Bus: 14, 27, 39A, 46A, 155
Luas: Green Line, Trinity

EUR
€–€€

W
stagshead.ie

Keep your eyes peeled on Dame Street for a mosaic of a stag's head on the pavement that points you in the direction of Dame Court. Featured in movies including *Educating Rita, A Man of No Importance*, and horror series *Penny Dreadful*, The Stag's Head is one of Dublin's most beautiful Victorian-era pubs. Low lighting, stained-glass windows, an imposing mahogany bar, and a majestic wall-mounted stag's head lend an elegant, Gothic vibe. But downstairs, in the 'Stag's Tail', there's a serious craic den. Regular storytelling events, live music sessions and comedy gigs pull in the crowds most nights. The pub serves a selection of classic Irish dishes from 1–7pm daily including beef and Guinness stew, fish pie, and its own take on a ham and cheese toastie – sourdough bread, Irish ham hock, Dubliner cheese and béchamel sauce.

The Temple Bar

Non-stop craic at one of Dublin's most photographed pubs.

47–48 Temple Bar, Dublin 2

Bus: 16, 37, 39, 39A, 46A, 70, 77A, 155, C4

Luas: Green Line, Westmoreland

EUR
€€

W
thetemplebarpub.com

Since you're going to strike a pose outside this pub and its famous sign – because Temple Bar, right? – you might as well duck inside to see what all the fuss is about.

Although a little pricier than other Dublin bars, The Temple Bar offers live music seven nights a week – plus, it has one of the largest selections of independent lagers, ales and stouts in the city. The whiskey selection really is something to shout about, too. The tidy collection includes over 400 Irish whiskeys, bourbons and Scotch whiskies, so take your time, settle in, enjoy the tunes, and soak up the craic.

Toners

The Baggot Street bar that stole a poet's heart.

139 Lower Baggot Street,
Dublin 2

Bus: 4, 18, 39, 70, 145
Luas: Green Line, Dawson

EUR
€

W
tonerspub.ie

Not only does Toners on Baggot Street claim to serve up one of the best pints of Guinness in Dublin, but it's also said to be the only pub in the city to have captured the heart of W.B. Yeats. Open since 1818, Toners exudes Victorian old-world charm, retaining many beautiful original features, including glass cabinets behind the bar and a traditional wooden snug area, which has changed little since Yeats's time. Out back, there's a lively and spacious beer garden that's a suntrap in the summer months and a welcoming heated outdoor space during the rest of the year.

Whelan's

A wonderland of live music on Wexford Street since 1989.

25 Wexford Street, Dublin 2

Bus: 15A, 16, 122
Luas: Green Line, Harcourt

EUR
€–€€

W
whelanslive.com

Sticky floors and sweaty crowds are all part of the rock'n'roll experience at Whelan's, the Wexford Street bar and venue where the likes of Ed Sheeran, Nick Cave and Arctic Monkeys have all made their mark over the years.

Whelan's layout is a vibe in itself – while the main room at the back stages sell-out shows and raucous indie DJ sets, the front bar is a buzzy, high stool and cosy turf fire situation. Visit on Christmas Eve and an impromptu singsong with Glen Hansard might be on the cards. Upstairs is a smaller venue that hosts silent discos and small, intimate gigs, and next door is Little Whelan's, a recently added bar and micro venue that holds just 50 people. Take your pick. A good time is guaranteed.

Pubs and Bars

Bar 1661

A poitín and cocktail bar in Dublin 7.

Tucked away just off Capel Street, this award-winning bar is named after the year that poitín (a highly potent traditional Irish spirit) was banned in Ireland. The menu features a range of poitín-infused libations as well as classic cocktails, non-alcoholic cocktails, and expertly crafted new takes on old favourites, like the Mad March Mule – a blend of Mad March Hare poitín, ginger, pale ale, and orange blossom. There is also an impressive selection of Irish whiskeys and gins to try, as well as a well-curated rum selection. Bar snacks are designed for sharing and include olives, oysters, and cheese and charcuterie boards.

1–5 Green Street, Dublin 7

Bus: 39, 39A, 69, 70, 145, C1, C2
Luas: Red Line, Jervis;
Green Line, Dominick

EUR
€€

W
bar1661.ie

The Cobblestone

A Smithfield pub renowned for its traditional Irish music sessions.

77 North King Street, Smithfield, Dublin 7

Bus: 26, 39, 83, 145, C1, C4
Luas: Red Line, Smithfield

EUR
€

W
cobblestonepub.ie

Run by Tom Mulligan, whose family has been playing music for five generations, this is a true Dublin treasure and one of the best places in the city to connect with authentic Irish culture.

While Dublin writer Brendan Behan once called himself 'a drinker with a writing problem', Smithfield pub The Cobblestone likes to think of itself as 'a drinking pub with a music problem'. This friendly, no-frills pub hosts traditional Irish music sessions seven nights a week including Na Píobairí (pipers seisiún) on the first Tuesday night each month and the Balaclavas session, which takes place every Wednesday in The Backroom. Led by music tutor Jacqui Martin, this class has been running for over 20 years and provides adults with the opportunity to learn traditional Irish music.

The Brazen Head

Stop by Dublin's oldest pub for a pint and a few tunes.

Based in the centre of Medieval Dublin, just a short stroll from Christ Church Cathedral and the Guinness Brewery, The Brazen Head is worth visiting for both its history and its live music tradition.

Officially Dublin's oldest pub (it dates back to 1198), The Brazen Head hosts nightly traditional Irish music sessions as well as its famous Sunday sessions, which take place weekly from 3.30–6.30pm. This is a popular venue with tourists all year round, but don't let that put you off – on a summer's evening, the cobblestone beer garden out front is a top spot to sink a pint.

20 Lower Bridge Street,
Usher's Quay, Dublin 8

Bus: 26, 39, 39A, 60, C4
Luas: Red Line, Four Courts

EUR
€€

W
brazenhead.com

John Kavanagh – The Gravediggers

Come for the Guinness, stay for the unique history and folklore.

---

1 Prospect Square, Glasnevin, Dublin 9

Bus: 40, 40D, 83, 155

EUR

€

Located next to Glasnevin Cemetery, The Gravediggers was founded in 1833 by John Kavanagh and at the time of writing, three generations of the same family are working side by side and the ninth generation are in the wings. Not only has the Kavanagh family preserved many of the bar's original features, but they have also upheld the tradition of no music, singing, or television in the bar. There is no shortage of entertainment, however. Ask any of the staff about ghostly goings-on and they'll be only too happy to tell you about the sharply dressed man who haunts the corner table or the secret hatch where workers from the cemetery would be passed sneaky pints of stout back in the day. Who can blame them? The Guinness here is legendary. If you drop in at lunchtime, they serve a very tasty traditional Dublin coddle, too – a slow-cooked, hearty stew made from bacon, sausage, potatoes, carrots and onions. Trust me, it's delicious.

The Abbey Tavern

Sink a pint at this rustic seaside bolthole.

---

28 Abbey Street, Howth

Bus: 6, H3
DART: Howth Station

EUR
€€

W
abbeytavern.ie

Located next to the ruins of St Mary's Abbey on Howth's Abbey Street, The Abbey Tavern dates back to the 16th century. It's every inch the seaside bolthole with its cut stone walls, flagstone floors, turf fires, and cosy decor. If you've just come from a hike around Howth, it's the perfect place to grab lunch and a pint – the seafood chowder is *chef's kiss*, and the vegan-friendly cauliflower wings are excellent.

Making a night of it? The pub also lays on a show in the evenings, which kicks off with a three-course dinner at 7.30pm, followed by traditional Irish music and dancing performances that wind down at 10.30pm.

Fitzgerald's

A friendly neighbourhood local that tips its hat to James Joyce.

---

11 Sandycove Road, Sandycove

/

Bus: 7, 7A, 45A, 59
DART: Sandycove and Glasthule

EUR
€

W
fitzgeraldsofsandycove.com

Part of Sandycove village life since 1861, Fitzgerald's is just a stone's throw from the Forty Foot and its landmark Martello Tower, which is now home to the James Joyce Tower & Museum. Fitzie's, as it's known locally, also pays homage to the writer with stained-glass windows that depict chapters from *Ulysses*, as well as literary posters, newspaper cuttings, and other memorabilia dotted around its walls. Fitzgerald's ticks all the boxes for service, pints and atmosphere, no matter what day you visit, but on Bloomsday (16 June), it's always a bit more extra, when locals and Joycean scholars congregate in their best Edwardian gear to raise a toast to their local hero.

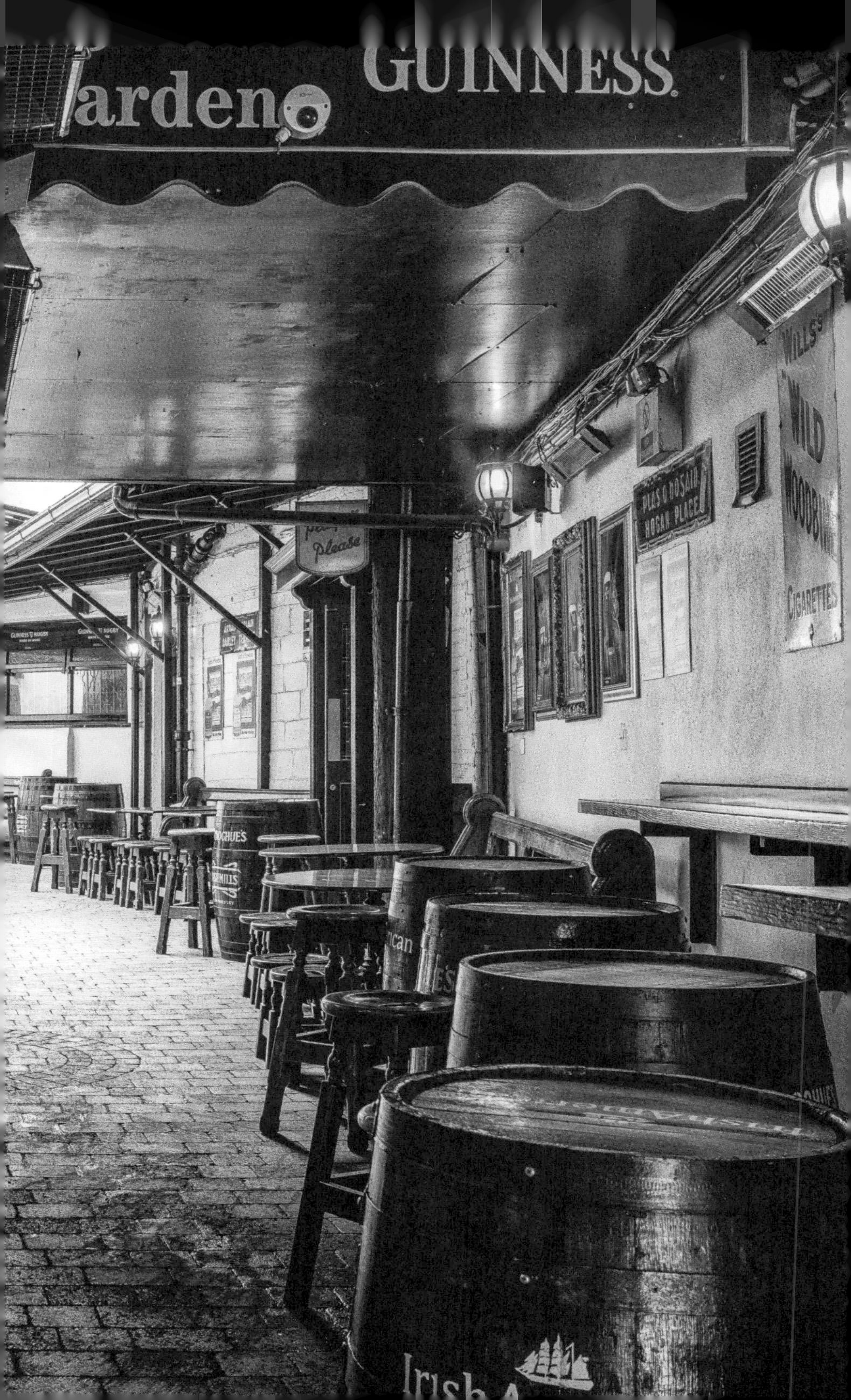
GUINNESS
Please
HOGAN PLACE
WILD
WOODBINE
CIGARETTES

CULTURAL
ATTRACTIONS

Between its UNESCO City of Literature status, Viking origin story, and well-known breweries and distilleries, Dublin is a cultural playground.

Understand Dublin's place on the world stage and follow in U2's footsteps by spending an afternoon at Windmill Lane Studios (see p. 135). Learn about the city's medieval past at the National Museum of Ireland (see p. 133). Discover more about Ireland's most celebrated writers and literary figures at MoLI (see p. 129). Get to grips with the history and heritage behind Gaelic games at Croke Park and GAA Museum (see p. 134). Go beyond the hall door and tour a Georgian house at 14 Henrietta Street, tracing its history over 300 years (see p. 123). Find out how to pull the perfect pint of Guinness and enjoy a bird's eye view of Dublin at the Guinness Storehouse (see p. 137). In these pages, you'll find some of the city's best museums, galleries and cultural attractions, each providing a unique insight into the Irish capital and its people.

14 Henrietta Street

Journey through 300 years of one Georgian property's history, from opulent townhouse to tenement dwelling.

Ever wondered what the walls of a Georgian house would say if they could talk?

A museum experience like no other, 14 Henrietta Street uncovers layer upon layer of history to reveal the fascinating story of a real Dublin Georgian townhouse.

From the opulence of an upper-class household in the 1740s to its descent into a 20th-century tenement, the museum traces the history of this redbrick house over 300 years.

Tenement houses were created in Dublin in the late 19th and early 20th centuries in response to swelling Dublin populations after the Great Famine and could be found throughout the north inner city, the Liberties, and the south docklands. Often, entire families were crammed into one room and houses were home to up to 100 people. Through the stories from the excellent tour guides and the authentically reconstructed rooms, you get a picture of what daily life was like in the tenements.

If, like me, you're interested in history, genealogy, or architecture, a visit to 14 Henrietta Street is a must.

9	🚃/🚌	**EUR**
14 Henrietta Street, Dublin 1	Bus: 1, 4, 9, 11, 13, 16, 38, 38A, 40, 46A, 83, 122, 140	€
W 14henriettastreet.ie	Luas: Green Line, Dominick or Broadstone	

Abbey Theatre

Catch a play or explore the history of Irish theatre.

26/27 Lower Abbey Street,
Dublin 1

Bus: 4, 7, 14, 27, 41, 46A
Luas: Red Line, Abbey Street;
Green Line, Marlborough

EUR
€–€€

W
abbeytheatre.ie

Founded in 1904 by poet and writer W.B. Yeats and dramatist Lady Gregory as a national theatre for Ireland, the Abbey Theatre was established during the height of Ireland's cultural revival as a venue 'to bring upon the stage the deeper emotions of Ireland'.

These days, the theatre still produces many of its plays in-house and attracts productions from around the world – check the theatre's programme online for upcoming shows. For anyone looking to find out more about the creative process, tickets to backstage tours can be booked online and provide an insight into the history of the theatre and the world of theatre production and design.

EPIC: The Irish Emigration Museum

Explore what it means to be Irish.

The CHQ Building, Custom House Quay, Docklands, Dublin 1

Bus: 14, 15, 27, 31, 32, 42, 43, 53, 130

Luas: Red Line, George's Dock

EUR
€

W
epicchq.com

Located close to the Dublin docks, where so many Irish people set sail for a new life, EPIC takes you on a journey that is both harrowing and uplifting. Through digital and interactive exhibits, the museum shares the wins and losses of those forced to leave Ireland and the adventures and struggles they experienced along the way.

The exhibit, highlighting the impact of Irish culture on fashion, music, sport, dance, film, food, politics and society around the world, is a real eye-opener. There's also an innovative 'whispering library' where you can pull talking books from a shelf to learn more about a number of notable Irish authors.

If you're keen to discover your Irish ancestry, it's possible to book a consultation with one of the genealogy experts in EPIC's Irish Family History Centre.

Tickets to EPIC can be booked online or from the ticket desk on arrival. The museum is open daily.

Cultural Attractions

Hugh Lane Gallery

Discover the world's
first public gallery of modern art.

Opened in 1933 as the Municipal Gallery of Modern Art, Dublin's Hugh Lane Gallery honours the vision of Cork-born art dealer Sir Hugh Lane, who established Dublin's Municipal Gallery of Modern Art in 1908, at a temporary location on Harcourt Street. At the time, it was thought to have been the first public gallery of modern art in the world. Sadly, Lane did not live to see the gallery find a permanent home, as he died tragically in 1915 on board the RMS *Lusitania*, off the west coast of Cork.

These days, the gallery hosts a diverse and exciting programme of temporary exhibitions, as well as a permanent collection of modern and Impressionist pieces from some of my favourite artists, including Manet, Monet, and Pissarro. Those who pay a visit can look forward to thought-provoking installations, a dedicated stained-glass room displaying Harry Clarke's masterpiece, *The Eve of St Agnes*, and the painstakingly preserved Francis Bacon Studio. Shipped from London in 1998, it includes every inch and detail of the artist's chaotic studio, from the walls, floor, door and ceiling down to the paintbrushes, slashed canvasses, and particles of dust.

Admission to the Hugh Lane Gallery is free but you're welcome to make a voluntary contribution at the kiosk upon entry. Closed Mondays.

Q		**EUR**
Charlemont House,	Bus: 7, 11, 13, 16, 38,	Free
Parnell Square North,	40, 46A, 123	
Dublin 1	Luas: Green Line,	**W**
	O'Connell Upper	hughlane.ie
	or Parnell;	
	Red Line, Abbey Street	

     Cultural Attractions

Book of Kells and Old Library

View a precious 9th-century manuscript and visit one of the world's most beautiful libraries.

The Old Library Building, Trinity College, College Green, Dublin 2

Bus: 27, 39, 39A, 46A, 145
Luas: Green Line, Trinity

EUR
€

W
tcd.ie/visitors/book-of-kells

Beautifully intricate and far smaller than you'd expect, the Book of Kells is one of Ireland's national treasures. The 9th-century manuscript is a gospel book and contains the four accounts of Christ's life that form the New Testament of the Bible. It was presented to Trinity College for safekeeping by the Bishop of Meath in 1661. It is housed in the Treasury in the Old Library, and visitors can view the book's ornate Latin text and detailed illustrations through a specially designed display case.

Entry to the Book of Kells also includes access to The Long Room – the spectacular Hogwarts-esque library that's home to over 200,000 of Trinity College's most precious books, as well as a rare original copy of the Proclamation of the Irish Republic.

As it is one of Dublin's most popular attractions, tickets to the Book of Kells and Old Library should be purchased online in advance. Open daily.

Museum of Literature Ireland (MoLI)

A modern, interactive museum celebrating Ireland's literary heritage.

UCD Naughton Joyce Centre,
86 St Stephen's Green, Dublin 2

Bus: 7, 11, 15, 16, 39A,
44, 46A, 140, 145, 155
Luas: Green Line,
St Stephen's Green

EUR
€

W
moli.ie

The lovechild of the National Library of Ireland and University College Dublin, Museum of Literature Ireland, or MoLI, is one of the newest additions to Dublin's museum scene. Housed in UCD's Naughton Joyce Centre in the historic Newman House, MoLI is a cleverly designed, vibrant and interactive space that celebrates living Irish writers as much as those from the past. Joyce's private notebooks, the 'Copy no. 1' first edition of *Ulysses*, as well as scale models and films recreating Dublin in Joycean times can be explored along with recordings of contemporary Irish writers and rotating exhibitions.

Beautifully landscaped gardens to the rear of the museum connect with the secret walled park in Iveagh Gardens, where two protected trees stand, one of which is an ash tree that James Joyce was photographed beneath on his graduation day.

Weather permitting, breakfast or lunch can be enjoyed on the garden terrace from The Commons, the museum's gourmet cafe run by Domini and Peaches Kemp.

Tickets for the museum can be booked online.

National Gallery of Ireland

*Explore Ireland's largest collection of art on
Merrion Square.*

What I love about the National Gallery of Ireland is that you can wander in at any time – no tickets or tours are necessary – and although some exhibitions carry a charge, the permanent collection is free. It's like the art belongs to you – and in a way, it kind of does. When the gallery first opened its doors in 1864, its premise was to provide a national collection for the nation to enjoy all year round.

The building itself is beautiful – its oldest wing, the Dargan Wing, dates from 1864. The Milltown Wing came next in 1903, while the Beit Wing was added in 1968 and the Millennium Wing in 2001.

There are approximately 14,000 works of art in the gallery, including the famous lost Caravaggio, *The Taking of Christ*, which was discovered casually hanging in a Jesuit house on Leeson Street in the 1990s. Other popular paintings from the permanent collection include Frederic William Burton's heart-wrenching *The Meeting on the Turret Stairs*, Jack B. Yeats's *The Liffey Swim*, Johannes Vermeer's *Lady Writing a Letter with her Maid*, and Daniel Maclise's epic *The Marriage of Strongbow and Aoife*.

Merrion Square West, Dublin 2; the gallery is also accessible via an entrance on Clare Street

Bus: 4, 7, 8, 15A, 15B, 39A, 46A, 145
Luas: Green Line, Dawson

EUR
Free; admission fee for special exhibitions

nationalgallery.ie

Cultural Attractions

National Museum of Ireland: Archaeology

Discover Dublin's Viking origins.

The National Museum of Ireland tells the story of Ireland from ancient times to the early modern period. For me, the standout exhibition is Viking Ireland, which explores life in Ireland and particularly Dublin during Viking times through artefacts discovered mainly during archaeological digs that took place in Dublin's Wood Quay in the 1970s and '80s. It is said to be one of the most comprehensive collections of excavated finds from an early medieval site anywhere in Europe, showing the Vikings in a whole new light and the contribution they made to Ireland culturally, economically, and politically.

Meanwhile, Glendalough: Power, Prayer and Pilgrimage looks at a very different medieval settlement – the monastic city of Glendalough, Co Wicklow, which was founded by St Kevin in the 6th century. The history of the sacred site is revealed in 26 objects – from a lady's leather shoe thought to have been lost in the 10th or 11th century to Viking coins discovered in the 1980s. Admission to the National Museum of Ireland is free. The museum is open daily.

		**EUR**
Kildare Street, Dublin 2	Bus: 4, 7, 7A, 11, 26, 27, 37, 38, 39, 39A, 40, 46A, 145, 155	Free
W		
museum.ie	Luas: Green Line, Dawson	

Croke Park and GAA Museum

Visit Ireland's Gaelic games HQ.

Jones' Road, Drumcondra, Dublin 3

Bus: 1, 11, 13, 16, 33, 40, 40B, 40D, 41, 41B, 41C, 44, 123

Train: Drumcondra

EUR

€

W

crokepark.ie/gaamuseum

The spiritual home of hurling and Gaelic football – and country musician Garth Brooks – Croke Park is the third largest stadium in Europe, with a capacity of 82,300. A tour of Croke Park and its GAA Museum gives you an insight into the evolution of Gaelic games from ancient times to the present. As part of the museum experience, you can view the original Sam Maguire and Liam MacCarthy Cups, visit the Hall of Fame exhibition, and put your hurling and Gaelic football skills to the test in the interactive games zone.

If you've got a head for heights, there's the option to see Croker and Dublin city from a whole new perspective by adding the stadium's skyline tour to your experience. From a platform suspended 17 storeys above Croke Park's pitch, you can take in panoramic views that stretch from the mountains to the sea.

Entry to the GAA Museum is included with the Croke Park Tour and museum access is also free for match ticket holders. The Kellogg's Skyline Croke Park Tour can be booked as an optional extra. Tickets for tours should be booked online in advance, as tour times may be adjusted on match days.

Windmill Lane Studios

Tour the studios where some of the world's biggest artists have recorded music.

Behind a blue and white – very accidentally Wes Anderson-esque – facade, some of the most incredible music of the last 40 years has been recorded. Named after its original location on Windmill Lane, the Ringsend Road recording studios have recently started welcoming visitors to the Art Deco building where U2, Kate Bush, The Rolling Stones, Spice Girls, and The Cranberries all laid down tracks. The unique visitor experience includes behind-the-scenes details about recording sessions that took place at the studios, a studio tour, and an overview of the recording and production process, plus the chance to mix your own session with the studio's virtual band. Tickets should be booked online in advance.

20 Ringsend Road, Docklands, Dublin 4

Bus: 47, 77A, C1, C2, C4
DART: Grand Canal Dock

EUR
€

W
windmilllanerecording.com

Guinness Storehouse

Visit the home of the black stuff.

There's no mistaking the official home of the black stuff ... The Guinness Storehouse is a seven-floor, state-of-the-art structure built around a central glass atrium in the shape of a giant pint glass. But just in case you're in any doubt, you can check out Arthur Guinness's original lease on the site – it's under the glass floor as you enter the lobby and confirms the 9000-year agreement.

The building might not be going anywhere fast, but the self-guided tour certainly puts you through your paces. From the brewing process and its history to the evolution of Guinness bottles and cans, a history of the Guinness family, and a nostalgia-filled floor dedicated to Guinness's epic advertising campaigns (my favourite bit), as well as a Guinness Academy teaching you how to pull the perfect pint, there's much to discover and explore before you reach the pièce de résistance – the Gravity Bar on the top floor, where you can take in 360-degree views of the city over a complimentary pint.

If you're interested in digging deeper into the history of Guinness – especially if you have family who once worked for the brewery – it's possible to arrange a visit to the Guinness Archive. The archive includes photos and personnel records from the 1880s to the early 2000s. Appointments for the Guinness Archive must be made online at least one week in advance.

Tickets to the Guinness Storehouse should be booked online in advance and include a complimentary pint of Guinness in the Gravity Bar. The Storehouse is open daily.

♀
St James's Gate, Dublin 8

Bus: 13, 123, G1, G2
Luas: Red Line, James's

EUR
€€

W
guinness-storehouse.com

Cultural Attractions

IMMA: Irish Museum of Modern Art

Discover thought-provoking artworks in a beautiful 48-acre setting in Kilmainham.

Royal Hospital Kilmainham, Military Road, Kilmainham, Dublin 8

Bus: 13, 40, 60, 123, G1, G2
Luas: Red Line, Heuston

EUR
Free

W
imma.ie

Located in the historic Royal Hospital Kilmainham building, within a 15 minute walk of both the Guinness Storehouse and Kilmainham Gaol, is the Irish Museum of Modern Art (IMMA). The collection focuses on pieces from 1940 onwards and includes portraits by Lucian Freud, as well as works by Roy Lichtenstein, Tracey Emin, and sculptor Barry Flanagan – his joyful, 15ft high bronze statue of a drumming hare stands at the main entrance to the museum.

As well as the museum, there is a 48-acre site to explore, including formal gardens and a beautiful cobbled internal courtyard where IMMA lays on free music concerts during the summer months. The Royal Hospital grounds are also a popular event venue – I've seen some amazing gigs here over the years.

Entry to IMMA's permanent collection is free. The museum closes on Mondays, except bank holidays.

Kilmainham Gaol

Moving and insightful tour of a historic Dublin prison.

Inchicore Road, Kilmainham, Dublin 8

Bus: 60, 69, C4, G1, G2
Luas: Red Line, Suir Road

EUR
€

W
kilmainhamgaolmuseum.ie

Opened in 1796 and considered the 'Bastille of Ireland', Kilmainham Gaol is one of Dublin's most haunting visitor attractions. The prison was decommissioned in 1924, but remains a foreboding place, its freezing cells evoking the fear and misery of the ordinary citizens, rebels, and political leaders who were incarcerated within its walls. In recent years, the building has become a popular film set, featuring in major movies including the Academy Award-nominated *In the Name of the Father*, *Michael Collins*, and *Paddington 2*.

Guided tours give an insight into the history of the prison and its inmates, including 14 leaders of the 1916 Rising, who were executed in the prison yard. One of the most poignant stories is that of Joseph Mary Plunkett and his fiancée, Grace Gifford, who were married in the prison chapel on 3 May 1916 just hours before Plunkett was executed for his role in the Easter Rising.

Entrance to Kilmainham Gaol is by guided tour only – advance booking is required.

Teeling Distillery

Get to the heart of the Liberties' whiskey-making tradition.

13–17 Newmarket, Dublin 8

Bus: 27, 56A, 77A, 151

EUR

€–€€

W

teelingdistillery.com

When the Teeling family opened their whiskey distillery in the Liberties in 2015, they reignited a spark that was first lit in 1782, when their ancestor Walter Teeling set up a craft distillery on Marrowbone Lane, just a stone's throw from the current distillery site.

There are several tour options on offer, with varying price points. For a decent understanding of the production process, I'd recommend the Teeling Trinity Tasting Tour. Not only does it give you an insight into the business of whiskey-making and the Teeling family history, but it also challenges your tastebuds to identify the subtle differences between small-batch, single-grain, and single-malt whiskeys.

All tours are fully guided and last approximately 60 minutes. Tickets should be purchased online in advance, as tours tend to book up fast.

Glasnevin Cemetery

Visit the final resting place of heroic Irish figures and explore the world's first cemetery museum.

Finglas Road, Glasnevin, Dublin 11

Bus: 4, 9, 40, 140, 155

EUR

€

W

dctrust.ie

From celebrated Irish political figures such as Daniel O'Connell, Éamon de Valera, Michael Collins, and Charles Stewart Parnell to poets and musicians like Brendan Behan and Luke Kelly, the gravestones of Glasnevin Cemetery tell the fascinating story of Irish history and culture over the past 200 years. Since 1832, around 1.5 million people have been laid to rest at the Victorian garden cemetery, which was established by Irish nationalist leader Daniel O'Connell as a place where people of all religions could bury their loved ones with dignity. Guided tours can be booked online and include access to the Visitor Centre – an indoor museum that explores funeral culture around the world and an exhibition that shares the stories of some of the cemetery's most interesting individuals. Guests of the tour also have the option to climb the 198 steps of O'Connell Tower.

Cultural Attractions

OUTDOOR
ADVENTURES

From hiking Howth's spectacular coastline and exploring the rugged natural wonders of the islands on the north and south coasts, to discovering rare and unusual flora in the beautiful, manicured gardens of Malahide Castle (see p. 159) and the National Botanic Gardens (pictured opposite, also see p. 155), outdoor adventures are never far away in Dublin. Even in the city centre, there are tranquil escapes to be found in St Stephen's Green (see p. 149), Iveagh Gardens (see p. 146), and Merrion Square (see p. 148), where a weekly outdoor art gallery has become one of the city's loveliest weekend fixtures. Plus, let's not forget Phoenix Park (see p. 153) – one of Europe's largest enclosed parks where you can spot fallow deer, step back in time to a Victorian Walled Garden (see p. 154), and take a cycling tour at your leisure. The city and its surroundings are yours to discover – this chapter gives an overview of the green spaces and outdoor pursuits that are within walking distance of the city centre or just a short journey away.

Iveagh Gardens

Experience the hidden charms of Dublin's 'secret garden'.

Clonmel Street, Dublin 2

Bus: 15, 16, 40, 155
Luas: Green Line, Harcourt

iveaghgardens.ie

Often referred to as 'Dublin's secret garden', Iveagh Gardens is a Victorian park less than half the size of St Stephen's Green. Tucked away behind a stone wall, there are lots of lovely and unusual features to discover, including fountains, a rose garden, and a spectacular cascade.

During the summer months, the gardens really come to life when marquees pitch up for boutique food, comedy, and music events. By far my favourite of these is the Live at The Iveagh Gardens series of summer concerts, when Irish and international acts take to the stage for sell-out, sunset gigs. It's a totally unique atmosphere, very much enhanced by the long stretch in the evenings.

Love Lane

*One for the 'gram in
Temple Bar.*

Love Lane, Temple Bar,
Dublin 2

Bus: 16, 27, 39, 39A, 46A,
77A, 155, C4

'Love the Lanes' is an initiative by Dublin City Council to spruce up the laneways that connect the streets around Temple Bar. Local artists have been commissioned to create bold and vibrant murals, turning the once drab alleys into open-air galleries.

Previously known as Crampton Court, 'Love Lane' is the artery that connects Essex Street with the Olympia Theatre on Dame Street and features a wall covered in tiles with inspirational quotes and lyrics from famous actors, musicians, and writers. Stories and messages by loved-up couples also feature on the tiles as part of artist Anna Doran's latest installation. Love this one: 'We're the perfect mix, just like an oul' Rockshandy.'

Outdoor Adventures

Merrion Square Park

Visit Oscar Wilde and enjoy an open-air art exhibit on Merrion Square.

Merrion Square, Dublin 2

Bus: 4, 7, 7A, 15A, 15B, 26
DART: Pearse Station

Once a private garden that was only accessible to key holders from the surrounding Georgian homes, Merrion Square Park is now one of Dublin's most popular public parks. Its most striking – and most photographed – feature by far is the sculpture of Oscar Wilde. Commissioned by the Guinness Group in 1997, the exquisite piece depicts a dapper Wilde, book in hand, casually reclining on a quartz boulder that faces his childhood home at 1 Merrion Square.

One of my favourite things about the park is its open-air art gallery, which is held every Sunday on the external railings. Most of the artists are full-time professionals and are happy to chat with you about their pieces.

St Stephen's Green Park

Explore the city centre's largest park.

St Stephen's Green, Dublin 2

Bus: 14, 15, 16, 37, 38, 39, 39A, 40, 44, 46A, 61, 70, 145, 155
Luas: Green Line, St Stephen's Green

W

ststephensgreenpark.ie

The people of Dublin have many reasons to be thankful to the Guinness family – St Stephen's Green Park is just one of their generous gifts to the city. In the years before Sir Arthur Edward Guinness bought the land, the green space was accessible only to wealthy nearby residents who had keys to the locked gates. After an extensive landscaping project was carried out by William Sheppard, the park was formally opened to the public in July 1880.

Today, the 22-acre site is the largest of the parks in Dublin's Georgian garden squares and is home to a number of interesting features, including a sensory garden for the visually impaired, an ornamental lake, the W.B. Yeats Memorial Garden, and the landmark Fusiliers' Arch at the Grafton Street corner, which commemorates Royal Dublin Fusiliers who died in the Boer War. Fifteen sculptures are located throughout the green featuring literary and revolutionary figures, including James Joyce, Countess Markievicz, and Theobald Wolfe Tone. A statue dedicated to Sir Arthur Edward Guinness can be found on the west side of the park. Free lunchtime concerts take place in the summer months.

Outdoor Adventures

Surfdock

Water-based fun on Grand Canal Dock.

Whether we're flinging ourselves into the icy depths of the Forty Foot or shivering our way along the canal on a paddle board, nothing gets in the way of Dubliners and our water-based fun. It must be our Viking heritage. If you're inclined to get involved in the latter, Surfdock has been on the go for 30 years, offering lessons in windsurfing and SUP from Grand Canal Dock. All equipment, including wetsuits, buoyancy aids, and helmets, is provided. Small group classes take place in the sheltered enclosed waters of Grand Canal Dock and are suitable for beginners. Classes should be booked online in advance.

South Dock Road,
Grand Canal Dockyard,
Ringsend, Dublin 4

Bus: 47, C1, C2
DART: Grand Canal Dock

EUR
€€

W
surfdock.com

Outdoor Adventures

Phoenix Park

Spot deer in one of Europe's largest urban oases.

Phoenix Park is north of the Liffey, and if you're playing along with Dublin's postcode system, you'd assume the park's address to have an odd postcode number. However, the park is officially recognised as Dublin 8 due to a historic preference by Phoenix Park residents for the James's Street (Dublin 8) postal sorting office.

Opened by the Duke of Ormond in 1662 as a Royal Deer Park, Phoenix Park became a public park in 1747. To this day, around 600 wild fallow deer still inhabit its green spaces – keep an eye out and you might be lucky enough to spot one in the wild. Covering 700 hectares, the park is one of the largest enclosed parks in any capital city in Europe and is a lovely place to explore by bicycle – bikes can be rented from Phoenix Park Bikes at the Parkgate Street entrance.

Within the Phoenix Park grounds you'll find Dublin Zoo; Áras an Uachtaráin – the President of Ireland's official residence; Farmleigh, a 78-acre estate and former historic home of the Guinness family; and the Phoenix Park Visitor Centre.

Phoenix Park, Dublin 8

Bus: 25, 26, 37, 38, 39, 46A, 70, 145
Luas: Red Line, Museum or Heuston

W

phoenixpark.ie

Outdoor Adventures

Victorian Walled Kitchen Garden

Step back in time to a garden within a park.

Phoenix Park, Dublin 8

Bus: 26, 46A, 145

W

phoenixpark.ie

Next to the Phoenix Park Visitor Centre is the Victorian Walled Kitchen Garden, which has been recently restored to its original layout and planted with soft fruit, vegetables, herbs, and cut flowers using organic principles. Gardening workshops take place in the garden on the second Saturday of each month, where you can learn about how to grow your own plants and produce.

Planning a picnic in the park? Phoenix Cafe is located beside the Victorian Walled Kitchen Garden and offers tea, coffee, soft drinks and a menu of organic and sustainably sourced treats, snacks, and sandwiches. Alternatively, picnic boxes can be ordered online from the cafe and picked up on the day of your visit. The Victorian Walled Kitchen Garden opens daily.

National Botanic Gardens

A green escape, 3km from Dublin city centre.

Glasnevin, Dublin 9

Bus: 4, 9, 83, 155

W

botanicgardens.ie

Located in Glasnevin, approximately 3km from Dublin city centre, the National Botanic Gardens was founded in 1795 and contains more than 15,000 plant species from around the world.

Along with rare and exotic plants, there are architectural wonders to admire – beautifully restored glasshouses including the Palm House, which dates back to 1883, and the Curvilinear Range, which was originally constructed in 1848.

The National Botanic Gardens hosts many workshops and events throughout the year and as part of its ongoing commitment to conservation, is developing a seed bank to conserve Irish native plant seeds for future generations.

The National Botanic Gardens is open daily. Admission is free.

Outdoor Adventures

Ireland's Eye

Spot seals and seabirds off the coast of Howth.

Located around 1km to the north of Howth Harbour, Ireland's Eye is a small rocky island famous for its monastic settlement and seabird sanctuary.

The monastery was founded around 700 AD by three monks who were the sons of Nessan, a prince of the Royal House of Leinster. A holy manuscript known as the Garland of Howth – now on display in Trinity College – is said to have originated here.

In keeping with the early 19th-century tradition, a Martello Tower was built on Ireland's Eye in 1804 to defend against potential attacks by Napoleon.

Ireland's Eye is both a Special Area of Conservation and a Special Protection Area. Seals can be spotted around the island, while the highest point, known as the Stack, is home to a range of seabirds, including guillemots, razorbills, fulmars, gulls, gannets, cormorants and occasionally, puffins.

Ferry trips around the island depart from the West Pier and take 15 minutes to reach the island. In the summer months, when conditions allow, it's also possible to disembark and explore the island for an hour or two. Ferry trips operate all year round.

📍	🚍 / 🚌	**EUR**
West Pier, Howth	Bus: 6, H3	€
	DART: Howth Station	

Outdoor Adventures

Malahide Castle and Gardens

Discover magic in Malahide.

Located around a ten minute walk from Malahide village, Malahide Castle and Gardens is an easy daytrip from Dublin city centre. The beautiful Gothic-style castle dates from the 12th century and was occupied by the Talbot family from 1185 until 1976. It's now open to the public, with all castle and garden tickets including entry into the castle, the botanical gardens, and fairy trail – an interactive 1.8km walk filled with fairy houses, sculptures and other enchanting gems. Alternatively, there are ticket options available that also include entry to the butterfly house – located inside the walled garden, it's the only butterfly house in Ireland, where you can discover 20 different stunning species. If you're visiting with children, there's a special magical history castle tour option which is geared towards little ears and includes entry to the butterfly house too.

An Avoca food market and cafe is located within the grounds with an outdoor terrace for lunch al fresco.

The castle and gardens run seasonal events throughout the year, including spooky ghost tours in autumn, a family-friendly festive lights experience in winter, as well as summer concerts, which have featured big names over the years, including Prince and Arctic Monkeys.

Tickets to Malahide Castle and Gardens can be purchased online or from the visitor centre. Advanced booking is recommended during the summer months.

9	🚆/🚌	EUR
Malahide Demesne, Malahide	Bus: 42, 102, H2 DART: Malahide	€

W

malahidecastleandgardens.ie

Dalkey Island

Wildlife and history galore on Dalkey Island.

Approximately 400 metres off the coast of Dalkey is a disarmingly beautiful green and rugged island. The island was originally known as Deilg Inis, meaning 'thorn island' in Irish. Vikings later called it Deilg-ei, the Normans Dalk-ei, and most recently it was anglicised to Dalkey Island. As you can probably surmise, Dalkey Island has seen a lot of action over the years. Archaeological evidence suggests the first settlement was established 6000 years ago. An interesting collection of ruins survive, including a stone church known as St Begnet's Church, dating back to the 10th century, and St Begnet's Holy Well, which is reputed to cure rheumatism. At the southern end of the island there's a Martello Tower which was constructed in the early 19th century to defend against French invasion.

Although no longer inhabited by humans, the island is home to a colony of seals, rabbits, and a herd of wild goats. In spring and summer, roseate terns flock to a small rocky outcrop to the north of the island known as Maiden Rock.

Boat trips are available from Coliemore Harbour throughout the year and can be arranged locally.

♀	♟/♟	**EUR**
Coliemore Harbour, Dalkey	Bus: 59 DART: Dalkey	€

Dillon's Park

Coastal picnic spot with spectacular views
of Dalkey Island.

Located uphill from Coliemore Road, this small neighbourhood park features picnic tables, benches, a winding pathway that slopes down to the rocky shoreline and even an ancient well, which was discovered by locals in 2016.

For me, its most striking feature by far is the spectacular view of Dalkey Island. Looking for all the world like a chunk of Connemara that has floated into Dublin Bay, its unexpected beauty stops you in your tracks.

Dillon's Park also plays an important role in the annual four-day Dalkey Book Festival, when it is transformed into a venue called the Seafront, welcoming writers and speakers from around the globe for lively conversations, live performances, and exclusive interviews.

Surprisingly quiet and uncrowded, the park is a lovely place to walk, take a picnic, or indeed photograph the island from the shore.

Coliemore Road, Dalkey

Bus: 59
DART: Dalkey

Outdoor Adventures

MARKETS AND EPICUREAN STOPS

Organic farmers' markets might be all the rage now, but markets have always been part of Dublin's social fabric. In medieval times, streets were named after the types of markets that took place in specific locations – for example, Fishamble Street is where the fish markets were, Cook Street is where bakers sold bread and pastries, and Ship Street near Dublin Castle was originally 'Sheep' Street, where historically, sheep were traded.

And then, of course, there's Molly Malone, the legendary fishmonger and heroine of Dublin's unofficial anthem. Today, you might say that her spirit lives on through the Meath Street and Moore Street market traders who not only deal in bargains but also dry wit and banter.

Weekly farmers' markets take place the length and breadth of the city – and beyond – while specialist bakeries, artisan food stores, and gourmet grocers are flourishing. This chapter features some of the best.

Moore Street Market

*A historic market in
Dublin 1.*

Moore Street, Dublin 1

Bus: 7, 13, 46A
Luas: Red Line, Jervis;
Green Line, O'Connell – GPO

Welcome to one of Dublin's oldest surviving
street markets – the traders of Moore Street
first set out their stalls in the 18th century.

After the Great Irish Famine of the
1840s, and subsequent economic decline
of the city, stall holders helped to provide
small rations of fruit, vegetables, fish,
chickens, and rabbits to families in need,
while neighbouring streets sold second-hand
clothes, old furniture, and household items.

Still in existence to this day, albeit on
a much smaller scale, the open-air market
runs Monday–Saturday and mostly sells
fruit and vegetables. Christmas wouldn't be
Christmas in Dublin without the Moore Street
traders hawking decorations and stocking
fillers on nearby Henry Street. Go to grab a
bargain and the 'last of the wrapping paper'.

Bread 41

Organic cafe and bakery serving freshly baked pastries, batch loaf, and sourdough breads.

41 Pearse Street, Dublin 2

Bus: 77A, C1, C2, C4
DART: Pearse Station

EUR
€

W
bread41.ie

Bread 41's location – tucked away beneath the Loopline Bridge on Pearse Street – makes it feel like a hidden gem. The organic bakery and cafe space is run by Eoin Cluskey, Ballymaloe Cookery School graduate and owner of Bread Nation – a bakery that specialises in long fermented breads and old-style processes.

Bread 41 is famous for its sourdough, rye breads, and excellent traditional Irish batch loaf – a tall loaf with soft white bread and a dark crust on the top and bottom. You'll also find delicious sweet and savoury pastries, including croissants and cinnamon buns.

At the weekends, the cafe serves an all-day brunch menu featuring tasty and creative options like croissant Benedict – poached eggs, bacon, hollandaise, spinach, chive, and croissant; kimchi pancake – house kimchi pancake, peanut rayu, coriander and a fried egg; as well as the signature Bread 41 breakfast sandwich – pudding, bacon, fried egg, bacon jam, wood-fired ketchup, and mixed leaves on sourdough bread. Coffee comes from local roaster 3fe.

Fallon & Byrne Food Hall

Epicurean delights on Exchequer Street.

11–17 Exchequer Street,
Dublin 2

Bus: 14, 15, 16, 27, 83, 140

EUR
€€

W
fallonandbyrne.com

If only all grocery shopping experiences were like that of Fallon & Byrne Food Hall. An antithesis to bland, cookie-cutter supermarkets, the food hall at Fallon & Byrne takes you on a little holiday – you have that same sense of novelty and delight at discovering new brands and interesting ingredients at every turn.

Fallon & Byrne's food hall stocks Irish and international artisan foods of all kinds – organic and exotic fruit and vegetables, baked goods, teas, coffee, sauces, cheeses, cereals, meats, poultry, seafood, and wines. There's also a selection of freshly prepared Fallon & Byrne ready meals that can be enjoyed at home. Service is excellent and counter staff are friendly, helpful, and knowledgeable.

Even more delights await in the basement – a wine cellar that stocks over 600 wines – while upstairs, in the dining room, head chef Owen Burns delivers an innovative menu based on the finest Irish and international produce.

Loose Canon Cheese & Wine

Natural wines by the glass, charcuterie boards, and elevated toasties.

---

29 Drury Street, Dublin 2

Bus: 14, 15, 16, 83, 140
Luas: Green Line, Trinity

EUR
€–€€

W
loosecanon.ie

It's fair to say Loose Canon would be a stunning addition to any street corner in Dublin city, but it's like the owners manifested the buzzy location on Drury Street. It simply belongs there.

Headed up by Brian O'Caoimh and Kevin Powell, Loose Canon launched on Drury Street in 2018. It was the perfect venture for the pair – Brian previously managed and worked in Parisian cafe Coutume and established a natural wine pop-up experience at the bar. Meanwhile, Kevin is a former cheesemaker with Corleggy Cheeses.

Loose Canon serves a selection of natural wines by the (beautifully illustrated) glass, curated cheeseboards, Irish charcuterie from Gubbeen, The Wooded Pig, and Broughgammon Farm, and gooey gourmet toasties seven nights a week.

Sheridans Cheesemongers

The destination shop in Dublin for artisan Irish and international cheeses.

11 South Anne Street, Dublin 2

Bus: 16, 39, 39A, 145, 155
Luas: Green Line, Dawson

EUR
€–€€

W
sheridanscheesemongers.com

Sheridans Cheesemongers has been indulging cheese-loving locals since the 1990s. The Sheridan brothers, Kevin and Seamus, started the business in a Galway market in 1995 and now run two branches of the shop – one from Dublin's South Anne Street, and another much larger shop on Churchyard Street in Galway, where they have a wine bar upstairs. The Dublin shop stocks a wide selection of cheeses as well as Sheridans-branded crackers, olives, and antipasti. The shop's green-and-white-packaged cheeses can also be found in gourmet food stores across Ireland.

Temple Bar Food Market

A lively Saturday market in Temple Bar.

Meeting House Square,
Temple Bar, Dublin 2

Bus: 11, 26, 27, 39, 39A, 46A, C2
Luas: Green Line,
Westmoreland

W

templebarmarkets.com

A feast for the eyes, belly, and soul awaits every Saturday from 9.30am–4pm at Temple Bar's Meeting House Square. The plaza transforms into a lively farmers' market filled with live music, street food stalls, and local and organic produce. Expect wholefoods from The Good Crop Company, artisan olive oils and antipasti from Lilliput Trading Co., seasonal fruit and vegetables from McNally Family Farm, cakes and treats from Gourmet Grub Bakery, a selection of raw milk handmade cheeses from Corleggy Cheeses, Indian curries from Delhi2Dublin, and meats from Broughgammon Farm.

Meanwhile, just a few paces away, you'll find new and second-hand books, CDs, and vinyl on Barnardo Square from 10.30am–5pm.

Markets and Epicurean Stops

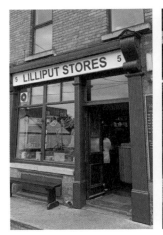

Lilliput Stores

*Gourmet grocer in
Stoneybatter.*

5 Rosemount Terrace,
Arbour Hill, Stoneybatter,
Dublin 7

Bus: 37, 39, 39A, 70

EUR
€–€€

W
lilliputstores.com

Named after the tiny island dreamt up by Dublin-born writer Jonathan Swift for his 1726 novel *Gulliver's Travels*, this small but perfectly stocked Stoneybatter shop has been trading in gourmet goods since 2007. Owned by Brendan O'Mahony and Aoife Cronin, Lilliput Stores specialises in Irish and Mediterranean foods – and they have cast their net far and wide to populate their shelves with quality products. In the back room of the shop, there's a lovely light-filled space where you can sit in and enjoy freshly prepared sandwiches, salads, cakes, pastries, and healthy, flavour-packed weekend brunches. Coffee comes from Imbibe roasters in Dublin 8. The shop's artisan hampers feature gourmet cheeses, Lilliput-branded crackers, and chutneys, and make an ideal gift.

Bretzel Bakery

Historic artisan bakery in Portobello.

1A Lennox Street, Dublin 8

Bus: 14, 15, 15A, 16, 83

EUR

€

W

bretzel.ie

Founded by a Russian-Jewish immigrant, Bretzel Bakery on Lennox Street has been a Portobello fixture since 1870. In recent years, current owner William Despard has transformed Bretzel into a thriving brand that now supplies artisan bread to restaurants, cafes, and retailers from a purpose-built base in Harold's Cross.

The original bakery shop on Lennox Street is still as charming as ever with its distinctive red and white awning and delivery bicycles. Open daily, it serves a range of freshly made sandwiches, coffees, pastries, bagels, and breads – pop in if you're in the neighbourhood or pick up a picnic to enjoy by the canal in Portobello.

Lennox Street Grocer

Fine foods, wines, and friendly welcomes in Portobello.

38 Lennox Street, Dublin 8

Bus: 14, 15, 15A, 16, 83, 122

EUR

€–€€

W

lennoxstreet.ie

With its vibrant, vintage-style shopfront and friendly wooden bench, Lennox Street Grocer looks right at home in its Portobello neighbourhood. Siblings Claire and Christopher Arnold opened the shop in 2020, and its shelves are stocked with fine wines, artisan jams and olive oils, as well as organic fruit and vegetables, meats, and cheeses. They also do a roaring trade in speciality coffee and sandwiches at lunchtime. Look out for the 'revolution ragu'. It's produced by The Upcycle Farm, who take leftover, nutrient-rich coffee grinds from Lennox Street Grocer to grow the oyster mushrooms for the vegan-friendly sauce. And keep an eye on their socials for news of wine tastings and events with artisan food producers.

Liberty Market

Bargains and banter on Meath Street.

Established in 1973 on Meath Street, Liberty Market is the ultimate Dublin bazaar, an indoor hotchpotch of stalls selling everything from clothing and shoes to plants, toys, books, wool, and homeware. Don't be afraid to haggle for a bargain – having the craic with the locals and stallholders is all part of the experience.

On Thursday, Friday, and Saturday, Meath Street itself comes to life with outdoor market traders selling discounted household essentials and other cheap and cheerful bits and pieces.

Meath Street, Dublin 8

Bus: 13, 123, G1, G2

W

libertymarket.ie

Markets and Epicurean Stops

Picado Mexican Pantry

Mexican flavours and feasts in Portobello.

44A South Richmond Street, Dublin 8

Bus: 14, 15, 15A, 16, 83

EUR

€–€€

W

picadomexican.com

Founded by Mexican Lily Ramirez-Foran and her Irish husband Alan Foran in 2011, Picado Mexican is a Portobello shop and cookery school where food lovers can learn about Mexico and discover authentic Mexican food and ingredients. Every product in the store has been carefully chosen by Lily and Alan, including spices, chillies, flour, sauces, crafts, and decorations. Cooking classes for small groups take place in the evening and offer guests the opportunity to learn how to make popular dishes such as tacos, tortillas, and tamales. It's a lovely communal experience – everyone sits down afterwards to enjoy their freshly prepared feast over drinks. The shop is closed on Mondays.

Howth Market

Weekend street food and artisan crafts in Howth.

3A Harbour Road, Howth

Bus: 6, H3
DART: Howth Station

W
howthmarket.ie

Popular with both tourists and locals, Howth Market is located opposite Howth DART station and just a stone's throw from Howth Harbour. The outdoor market is open on Saturdays, Sundays, and Bank Holiday Mondays and features around 25 stalls selling a selection of organic produce, freshly baked goods, handmade jewellery, artisan knitwear, and homeware. There is also a good selection of street food stalls serving a range of snacks, including churros, pizza by the slice, dumplings, noodles, hotdogs, and seafood chowder – enjoy on the go or pull up a seat at one of the many picnic benches. The market's Amore ice-cream parlour and Bodega speciality coffee shop open daily.

Markets and Epicurean Stops

People's Park Market, Dún Laoghaire

A Sunday market by the sea.

People's Park, Dún Laoghaire

Bus: 7, 7A
DART: Sandycove and Glasthule

Over 50 market vendors roll into the People's Park in Dún Laoghaire every Sunday from 11am–4pm, bringing a unique buzz and an eclectic range of produce, from artisan cheeses to gluten-free bread, chocolates, jams, organic fruit and vegetables and coffee, plus jewellery, handmade soaps, crafts, and paintings. Ethnic street food stalls are located at the nearby LexIcon – the choice of food is diverse and includes Italian, French, Indian, Greek, Pakistani and Middle Eastern.

The People's Park has been open to the public since 1890 and features a Victorian gate lodge and an elegant pavilion-style tearoom, which now houses a cafe and outdoor terrace – its sea views attract both locals and daytrippers.

Killruddery Farm Market

A Saturday market within the grounds of Killruddery House and Gardens.

Killruddery Farm Market is an easy Saturday daytrip from Dublin. Taking place in the Horse Yard within the grounds of Wicklow's spectacular Killruddery House and Gardens country estate, the outdoor market features organic vegetables from An Tairseach, Middle Eastern street food from What the Falafel, pastries and cakes from Day's Kitchen, hand-poured candles by Mowtini, leather goods by Wicklow-based Turas Leather, ceramics by Maple Tree Pottery, scented lavender products, and delicious sweet and savoury crepes from The Crepe Box.

Killruddery Horse Yard,
Killruddery House & Gardens,
Southern Cross Road,
Killruddery Demesne East,
Bray, Co Wicklow

DART: Take the DART to Bray and the 184 or 84 bus to Vevay Road.

Artisan wood-fired pizzas are also available in the Horse Yard, made using ingredients produced within the 800-acre estate.

The market takes place every Saturday from 10am–4pm. Entry to the market is free.

W
killruddery.com

Markets and Epicurean Stops

SHOPPING

From tweed caps and woven blankets to locally designed knitwear, hand thrown pottery, art, jewellery and glassware, Ireland is home to some of the world's most beautifully crafted fashion and homeware – and Dublin is Ireland's shop window. In the Irish capital, you'll encounter homegrown labels transforming traditional linens and textiles into stylish contemporary pieces, as well as high-end department stores and boutiques where you can shop for gifts, or a special memento of your trip to Dublin.

Explore concept stores like Temple Bar's Scout (see p. 199) and Indigo & Cloth (see p. 195), browse luxury Irish design in Avoca (see p. 189), STABLE of Ireland (see p. 200), and Irish Design Shop (see p. 196), discover locally crafted treasures by Chupi (see p. 191) in Powerscourt Townhouse Centre, or peruse high fashion in Brown Thomas (see p. 190) – Dublin's streets are filled with innovative brands and independent shops. This chapter looks at the city's most unique and inspiring places to find quality clothing, books, homeware and more.

Arnotts

Ireland's oldest and largest department store.

---

12 Henry Street, Dublin 1

Bus: 4, 7, 7A, 13, 38, 46A, 123, 140
Luas: Red Line, Jervis;
Green Line, O'Connell – GPO

W

arnotts.ie

Part of Henry Street's history since 1843, Arnotts features seven floors of luxury fashion, accessories, beauty, toys, books, furniture, and homeware. This department store holds a special place in the heart of Dubliners, especially at Christmastime, when its windows are transformed into magical winter wonderlands.

Throughout the year, Arnotts is a great place to discover emerging Irish brands and is renowned for its innovative and eclectic pop-up collections. It's also a great spot for those in search of sustainable options – you'll find a range of pre-loved designer accessories on the ground floor, as well as a handy repair and restoration service for shoes and trainers that require a bit of TLC. Fancy a spot of pampering during your shopping trip? The in-house hair and nail salons offer a full range of treatments and services.

Clerys

Recently revamped department store with a much-loved clock.

27 O'Connell Street Lower, Dublin 1

Bus: 7B, 38, 38A, 46A, 140
Luas: Green Line,
O'Connell – GPO;
Red Line, Abbey Street

After a recent transformation project, landmark O'Connell Street department store Clerys has emerged as the Clerys Quarter, a state-of-the-art retail and hotel space featuring a rooftop bar.

Clerys first opened its doors in 1853 as McSwiney, Delaney & Co. and was one of the first purpose-built department stores in the world. The building (and its famous clock) conjures happy memories for generations of Dubliners. From the 1940s to 1970s, the first floor housed a ballroom, complete with a full-time orchestra, which hosted nightly dances. Many a romance started on the Clerys dancefloor – and so began a tradition of couples arranging to meet their partners on O'Connell Street at the entrance to the department store beneath Clerys' clock. To this day, Dubliners still consider the Clerys clock a landmark meeting point.

Article

Gorgeous homeware in historic surroundings on South William Street.

Powerscourt Centre, South William Street, Dublin 2

Bus: 7A, 13, 14, 15, 16, 39, 39A, 46A, 155
Luas: Green Line, St Stephen's Green

W

article.ie

Housed on the ground floor of Powerscourt Townhouse, a dollhouse-like Georgian building on South William Street, Article offers a carefully curated selection of homeware, gifts, and small furniture items. Article opened in 2010 in the space once occupied by Lord Powerscourt's dressing room, and the shopping experience is as much about admiring the historic surroundings as it is about browsing the collection on display. From polished floorboards underfoot to elaborate ceiling plasterwork that dates from 1780, it's a truly beautiful and unique setting. On the shelves, you'll find woollen throws, candles, books, stationery, and prints, many of which are Irish designed. The collection is updated regularly, so if you've got your eye on something, make sure you snap it up.

Avoca

Homespun creations across seven floors.

11–13 Suffolk Street, Dublin 2

Bus: 7A, 16, 27, 39, 39A, 155
Luas: Green Line, Trinity

W
avoca.com

And the award for cosiest shop in Dublin goes to Avoca Suffolk Street. Over seven levels, the mini department store crams in beautiful throws, scarves, and baby blankets – woven in Avoca's Co Wicklow mill, as well as a selection of outdoor clothing, jewellery, books, kitchenware, and gift items. In the basement, there's a food market and coffee shop where you can pick up sweet treats, Avoca-branded ready meals, or a latte to go. If you fancy staying a while longer, hop in the lift to the top floor, where Suffolk Street Café serves breakfast, lunch, and a very tempting selection of cakes.

Brown Thomas

Luxury designer labels over five floors on Grafton Street.

88–95 Grafton Street, Dublin 2

Bus: 14, 27, 39, 39A, 145, 155
Luas: Green Line, Dawson

W

brownthomas.com

Brown Thomas is to Grafton Street what Selfridges is to London's Oxford Street – it's luxury shopping, but with a high-fashion edge. Home to a dizzying range of designer brands, BTs has been kitting out fashion-forward Dubliners since 1849, when it started out as a haberdashery and draper. The store continues to reinvent itself. These days, over five floors, you'll find beauty products, luxury jewellery and watches, designer clothing, bags and accessories, homeware, and a restaurant on the top floor that serves a rather swanky afternoon tea. Got an eye for a bargain? Brown Thomas's post-Christmas sales are literally a 'handbags at dawn' situation – serious shoppers have been known to queue from the early hours to get their mitts on heavily reduced designer goods. Sharpen those elbows.

Chupi

Handcrafted jewellery and sustainable sparklers in Powerscourt Townhouse.

Top Floor, Powerscourt Centre, South William Street, Dublin 2

Bus: 7A, 13, 14, 15, 16, 39, 39A, 46A, 155
Luas: Green Line, St Stephen's Green

W
chupi.com

Located on the top floor of the historic Powerscourt Townhouse, Chupi – founded by Chupi Sweetman in 2013 – is a treasure chest of thoughtfully designed and beautifully handcrafted jewellery. Each piece is created in Ireland using 100 per cent recycled gold, and diamonds are lab-grown, recycled, or ethically sourced.

Pieces are modern with an antique twist. The brand is known for its collectible, stackable rings and interesting selection of grey diamonds.

As a gift idea, I love Chupi's hand-illustrated gift coin – each limited-edition coin is engraved with a unique code that can be used online or in-store to purchase or go towards a piece of fine jewellery.

Shopping

Designist

A cleverly curated collection of Irish designed gifts and homeware.

---

68 South Great George's Street, Dublin 2

Bus: 9, 14, 15, 15A, 16, 83

W

shop.designist.ie

Designist was set up by Barbara Nolan and Jennie Flynn in 2010 with the aim of offering gorgeous well-designed products at affordable price points. Collaborating with Irish and international designers, they've come up with a cleverly curated collection – everything in shop retails for under €100 – from homeware and stationery to books and prints.

When it comes to gifts, its range of books is especially impressive. There are lots of interesting non-fiction titles by Irish authors and some very nice coffee table books. Equally impressive is the dedicated children's books section filled with fun, colourfully illustrated storybooks and Irish-themed fairytales.

Hodges Figgis

Historic bookshop selling over 70,000 titles.

56–58 Dawson Street, Dublin 2

Bus: 4, 7, 7A, 11, 26, 37, 38, 39, 39A, 46A, 145, 155
Luas: Green Line, Dawson

hodgesfiggis.ie

Dating back to 1768, Hodges Figgis is the oldest bookstore in Ireland and is thought to be the third oldest in the world. It has strong literary connections, too, and is famously mentioned in James Joyce's *Ulysses*: 'She, she, she. What she? The virgin at Hodges Figgis' window on Monday looking in for one of the alphabet books you were going to write.'

At the time of *Ulysses*, the shop was located on Grafton Street but moved to Dawson Street in 1992. It's the Dawson Street location that inspired Sally Rooney to set an entire chapter of *Conversations with Friends* in the store.

It's easy to see the appeal. Inside, a central staircase with decorative cast-iron rails brings the drama, while bookshelves wrap themselves around three floors, showcasing just about every category of book – there are over 70,000 titles to explore. Friendly and knowledgeable staff are on hand to provide recommendations or advice if you're looking for a particular book or need help choosing.

Shopping

Howbert & Mays

Picture-perfect garden shop on Clare Street.

16 Clare Street, Dublin 2

Bus: 4, 7, 7A, 15A, 15B, 26, 39, 39A
DART: Pearse Station

W
howbertandmays.ie

Occupying the striking Clare Street building that once housed Greene's Bookshop, Detroit native Anthea Howbert and her husband Tig Mays have created a garden shop with instant kerb appeal. From the inviting display of small plants and flowers to the distinctive glass canopy and pea-green facade, Howbert & Mays is about as Instagram-ready as it gets. On the ground floor, you'll find an urban oasis – two separate rooms filled with leafy houseplants, kitchen herbs, seeds, spring bulbs, ceramics, gardening accessories, greetings cards, and gift items. Upstairs, there's a range of soft furnishings and homeware. Staff are friendly, knowledgeable, and ready to advise.

Indigo & Cloth

Bringing speciality coffee and sustainable fashion to Temple Bar since 2007.

9 Essex Street East,
Temple Bar, Dublin 2

Bus: 16, 27, 39, 39A,
46A, 77A, 155, C4
Luas: Green Line,
Westmoreland

W
indigoandcloth.com

One part coffee bar, one part clothing and lifestyle store, Indigo & Cloth has been bringing speciality coffee and slow, sustainable fashion to Temple Bar since 2007. Exposed bricks, wooden benches, and cement floors add a workshop aesthetic to the ground floor, where the coffee magic happens – the house roast is sourced from Bailies in Belfast, while guest roasters rotate twice a year. On the first and second floors, you'll find an eclectic range of clothing brands from Europe, the US, and further afield, many of which are exclusive to Ireland. On the top floor, there's 'The Studio', a multifunctional space that hosts events, design studios, and artist collaborations.

Irish Design Shop

A modern take on Irish heritage crafts.

41 Drury Street, Dublin 2

Bus: 14, 15, 16, 77A, 83
Luas: Green Line, Trinity

W

irishdesignshop.com

Set up in 2008 by jewellers Clare Grennan and Laura Caffrey, Irish Design Shop celebrates modern Irish design and heritage crafts. Reclaimed wood, laminated birch ply, and concrete floors create a cosy, earthy aesthetic in the shop. But the standout feature is most definitely the functioning jeweller's workbench, where customers can watch original jewellery pieces being crafted for Irish Design Shop's jewellery line, Names. Browsing through the store, you'll encounter a rich and varied selection of products from over 50 makers, including jewellery, knitwear, candles, books, blankets, ceramics, and glassware. Clare and Laura also regularly collaborate with Irish designers on exclusive projects and products.

Kilkenny

Irish designs, gifts, and homeware on Nassau Street.

6 Nassau Street, Dublin 2

Bus: 4, 7, 7A, 11, 37, 38, 39, 39A, 155
Luas: Green Line, Dawson

kilkennyshop.com

Located just a short stroll from the National Gallery of Ireland, Kilkenny has been championing Irish craft and design for over 50 years and is home to Ireland's largest collection of Irish designs – many leading Irish designers, including Orla Kiely, Chupi, and Rebeka Kahn, started out at Kilkenny. If you're looking for a present or a memento to bring home, it's pretty much a one-stop shop for gifts – from gorgeous Dublin-made Rathbornes Candles to tweed caps handwoven in Killarney and wool blankets from Donegal to jewellery, homeware, children's books, framed paintings and prints, there's something uniquely Irish for every generation. Upstairs is a lovely light-filled cafe serving breakfast, lunch, and artisan cakes, plus gorgeous views of Trinity College.

Musicmaker

Rocking Exchequer Street since 1986.

29 Exchequer Street, Dublin 2

Bus: 14, 15, 16, 27, 83, 140

W

musicmaker.ie

Musicmaker has been attracting local musicians and world-famous talent since it opened its doors on Exchequer Street in 1986. And it's easy to see why. There are electric guitars for days, a drum skin collection signed by rock legends including The Edge and Blondie, plus amazing staff who eat, breathe and live music. In the basement, you'll find The Drumgeon – Musicmaker's brilliantly named drum department. It features the largest cymbal collection in Ireland and has famously also hosted a number of random underground gigs with some of the industry's most celebrated drummers. Drop in for the craic – you never know who you might meet.

Scout

Style and substance in Temple Bar.

5 Essex Street West,
Temple Bar, Dublin 2

Bus: 15, 16, 26, 27, 39, 145, C4, G2

W

scoutdublin.com

When Wendy Crawford opened Temple Bar's Scout in 2014, the aim was to curate a range of vintage clothing and one-off pieces sourced in Paris and Berlin. Since then, that vision has evolved and pivoted towards contemporary labels that have a heritage feel – products that are beautiful, functional, and made to last. These days in Scout, you'll not only find timeless, quality clothing, but also a fine selection of locally produced homeware and textiles. The space has been recently refurbished, too, with antique cabinets, tables, and shelving showcasing the shop's range of fragrant Irish-made candles, Scandinavian fashion labels, locally produced prints, sustainable skincare, scarves, bags, and accessories.

STABLE of Ireland

Stylish and luxurious Irish fashion and homeware.

Unit 2, Westbury Mall,
Balfe Street, Dublin 2

Bus: 27, 39, 39A, 70, 155
Luas: Green Line,
St Stephen's Green

W

stableofireland.com

Lifestyle brand STABLE of Ireland was founded by Francie Duff and Sonia Reynolds in 2015. They set out to reimagine Irish textile traditions and have created stylish and luxurious homeware and garments that can be enjoyed every day. In their Westbury Mall shop – just off Grafton Street – you'll find clothing, accessories, and homeware created using Irish linen, wool, cashmere, and alpaca.

The space itself is small and welcoming, with a colour palette that channels Irish mountains, coasts, and countryside. Antique display cabinets were sourced from a family haberdashery store in Wexford and printed textiles add pops of colour to the whitewashed walls.

The store's STABLE-branded linen products, including scarves, napkins, handkerchiefs, and their signature swim towels woven with Huck linen, make excellent gifts.

April and the Bear

A chic, eclectic interiors shop in Rathmines.

213 Rathmines Road Lower, Dublin 6

Bus: 15, 18, 83

W

aprilandthebear.com

Founded by former fashion buyer Siobhan Lam, April and the Bear is one of Dublin's most eclectic interiors shops. From custom-made mid-century furniture to Irish-made candles, prints, stationery, and coffee table books, the cheerful collection is carefully curated to put a smile on your face. As well as interesting and unique finds, the brand also makes a conscious effort to work with sustainable suppliers and local creatives. As a lover of art, furniture, and all things interior design, this shop has a special place in my heart – since the days of its original spot in Temple Bar, I've picked up some amazing coffee table books and prints here over the years.

Shopping

Arran Street East

Sustainable homeware and workshops in Smithfield.

Founded in 2015, Arran Street East is a pottery and weaving studio based in Smithfield. The studio's creations are influenced by the natural colours of the produce in the nearby Victorian fruit market.

All textiles and ceramics on sale in the shop are made by hand in a sustainable way, and no two items are the same. If you'd like to have a go yourself, there are year-round workshops and one-day classes where you can try weaving on a loom, get to grips with clay, or learn how to throw a pot on the pottery wheel. Classes can be booked in advance online.

43–44 Arran Street East, Dublin 7

Bus: 26, 37, 39, 39A, 70, 83, 145
Luas: Red Line, Jervis or Smithfield

W
arranstreeteast.ie

Jam Art Factory

A temple to Irish art and design in the Liberties.

64–65 Patrick Street, Dublin 8

Bus: 13, 27, 123, G1, G2

W

jamartfactory.com

Located between Christ Church and St Patrick's Cathedrals, Jam Art Factory is an independent gallery and design shop founded by brothers John and Mark Haybyrne in 2011. Their motto is: 'Design makes you happy, Irish design makes you happier.'

Inside, you'll find jewellery and ceramics as well as illustrations, old Irish maps, and vibrant limited-edition prints by Irish artists including Tara O'Brien, Claudine O'Sullivan, Fuchsia MacAree, Jacob Stack, and Maser. Many of the works reference or feature locations in Dublin and Irish themes, and make brilliant, beautiful gifts or souvenirs, especially if you or someone you know has a special grá (meaning 'love' in Irish) for a particular place in Ireland.

Surround

A stylish embrace
in Howth.

---

3 Main Street, Howth

Bus: 6, H3
DART: Howth Station

W
surround.ie

Walking into Surround, you encounter beautiful homewares, fashion, art, and books at every turn. And it's easy to see why – the shop is owned and managed by award-winning interior designer Naomi Keatley. With over 20 years' experience in transforming living spaces, Naomi brings together an eclectic range where cosy cashmere hats and scarves sit side-by-side with cosmetics sourced from Scandinavia and colourful prints featuring Howth and other nearby towns and villages in North Dublin.

The shop also hosts Naomi's interior and event design business. While you're shopping for gifts or souvenirs, browse the selection of fabric and wallpapers or get design inspiration and advice for your next home improvement project.

Seagreen

A luxury concept store by the sea.

6A–7A The Crescent,
Monkstown

 /

Bus: 4, 7A
DART: Salthill and Monkstown

W
seagreen.com

Inspired by European and US concept stores, founder Sarah Gill brought luxury lifestyle boutique Seagreen to the charming seaside village of Monkstown in 2006. Take your time to explore – the elegant decor and clever layout make the space feel like a chic apartment. From Irish-designed jewellery to chic French clothing labels, gorgeous scented candles, high-end perfumes, cosmetics, and stylish coffee table books, Seagreen's edit delivers the perfect collection, whether you're shopping for a gift, on the hunt for something decorative for your home, or looking for an investment piece for your wardrobe. Staff are friendly, attentive, and ready to beautifully wrap whatever you purchase.

DAYTRIP:
BELFAST AND
THE CAUSEWAY COAST

Discover the history of the world's most famous ship – the Titanic, learn about Belfast's troubled past, toast the city's renaissance, and travel to the nearby Antrim Coast to discover mythical landscapes.

The beating heart of Northern Ireland, there is much to admire about Belfast, not least the city's resilient spirit. Understand more about its turbulent – and very recent – past by taking the **Belfast Black Cab Tour** (touringaroundbelfast.com), which stops at key locations related to 'the Troubles', the period of sectarian violence that ran from about 1968–1998. There's also the opportunity to write your own message of positivity on one of the 'peace walls' that separate Catholic and Protestant areas.

Since 2012, **Titanic Belfast** has been sharing the history of the RMS *Titanic*, which was constructed in Belfast's Harland & Wolff shipyard and launched from the nearby slipways. The self-guided tour takes you on a sensory journey by recreating the sights, sounds and smells passengers experienced on board as well as the stories of the workers who built the ship. Allow two hours to appreciate the memorabilia, artefacts, and immersive experience, The Pursuit of Dreams. To see what makes modern Belfast tick, make your way to the **Cathedral Quarter**, a vibrant cobblestoned neighbourhood filled with street art, bars, restaurants, outdoor terraces and cultural attractions.

Head north from the city to the **Antrim Coast** and the **Giant's Causeway** – a geological wonder featuring around 40,000 hexagonal-shaped basalt columns of varying heights. According to legend, these are the remains of a bridge to Scotland built by Irish warrior and giant Finn McCool. Enraged by his Scottish rival Benandonner's claim to Ireland, he is said to have thrown boulders into the sea and challenged him to a duel.

Around 13km/8 miles from the Giant's Causeway is **Carrick-a-Rede Rope Bridge**, suspended 100ft above the Atlantic. It was originally constructed by salmon anglers in 1755 to link the mainland to Carrick-a-Rede Island. Today, visitors can tackle the 20 metre crossing or set out on the 2km coastal walk which offers views of Rathlin Island, Scotland, and Carrick-a-Rede. Along the way, you might also spot guillemots, razorbills, kittiwakes, and fulmars.

GETTING THERE

Approximate time and distance from Dublin: two hours (165km/102 miles).
Day tours: Wild Rover Tours (wildrovertours.com) offers a Dublin to Belfast day tour that includes a Black Taxi or Titanic Experience Tour, Antrim coastal drive, the Giant's Causeway, and Dunluce Castle.
By bus: Aircoach (aircoach.ie) provides a service between Dublin city centre and Belfast city. The journey time is approximately one hour and 55 minutes.
By train: A Dublin to Belfast service operated by Irish Rail (irishrail.ie) departs from Dublin Connolly and takes just over two hours.
Driving: Take the M1 from Dublin following signs for Belfast. Transition to A1 at the border.

Daytrip

DAYTRIP:
GLENDALOUGH AND WICKLOW
MOUNTAINS NATIONAL PARK

Glendalough or Gleann Dá Loch, which translates as 'valley of the two lakes', is just over an hour's drive from Dublin. Pack your walking boots for a scenic hike, explore the medieval monastic settlement, or simply take in the views and photograph the stunning landscapes.

With its calm, (astoundingly) beautiful glacial valley setting, **Glendalough** in Co Wicklow is exactly the type of place you might travel to if you were seeking spiritual enlightenment. Indeed, this sense of remote serenity is said to be what inspired St Kevin to establish a monastery here in the 6th century. Reminders of the **Monastic City** that once stood in the space are scattered across the glen, with ruins dating from the period between the 6th and 12th centuries. Some of the most impressive structures include a 30 metre high round tower, medieval stone churches, and St Kevin's Bed, an artificial cave cut into the cliff face above the Upper Lake, where it's thought that St Kevin lived and prayed.

Covering an area of 20,000 hectares, **Wicklow Mountains National Park** is remarkable for a few reasons. Not only is it Ireland's largest national park, but it's also the only national park in the country that's not located in the West of Ireland. Within the park you'll find deciduous and coniferous woodland areas – sessile oak, ash, Scots pine, and hazel are in abundance. The area is also a unique habitat for wildlife – goats, peregrine falcons, red squirrels, deer, and kestrels are just some of the creatures that have made their home here.

There are nine designated walking trails in Glendalough. Details of the trails can be found at nationalparks.ie. For a gentle 3km/2 mile walk, the **Green Road** is an easy, mostly flat loop trail that winds its way through Glendalough oak woodlands before leading you to the edge of the Lower Lake, where you can take in spectacular views of the valley.

Each one of the nine waymarked walks begins and ends at the National Park Information Office, close to the Upper Lake – staff are happy to answer any questions you might have about the routes and help you choose the most suitable option for your interests and ability.

GETTING THERE

Approximate time and distance from Dublin: one hour (51km/31 miles).
Day tours: Paddywagon Tours (paddywagontours.com) offers a half-day tour that departs from Dublin city early in the morning and gives visitors two hours to explore Glendalough and the Monastic City.
Driving: From Dublin take the N11/M11 south to Kilmacanogue village, then take the slip-road from the N11 and follow the R755 to Laragh village. From there follow the main road to reach Glendalough.

DAYTRIP:
IRISH NATIONAL STUD
& GARDENS

Take a stroll through a calming oasis, find out more about Ireland's horse-racing heritage, meet future champions and living legends, and see if you have what it takes to train a racehorse.

Just a short drive west of Dublin brings you to the vast, open grassy plains of Co Kildare. Known as the centre of Ireland's thoroughbred horse industry, it's here that you'll find the **Irish National Stud & Gardens**.

The history of the popular attraction can be traced back to 1900, when the lands around Tully were purchased by wealthy Scottish businessman Colonel William Hall Walker and developed into a stud farm. Soon Walker became one of the most successful and respected horse breeders in the industry, celebrating victory at the Epsom Derby in 1909 with Tully-bred Minoru.

Embracing the Edwardian trend of Japanese-inspired gardens, from 1906 to 1910, Walker worked with Japanese master horticulturist Tassa Eida to create a **Japanese Garden** on the Kildare site. Filled with stone lanterns, statues, a magnificent red 'Bridge of Life', mature bonsai trees, and an authentic tea house shipped from Japan, the gardens proved quite the spectacle.

Today, the original design of the gardens has been retained – visitors follow a carefully laid out trail that conveys the 'Life of Man' from the 'cave of birth' to the 'gateway of eternity'. In 1999, an additional attraction was added, **St Fiachra's Garden**. Designed by award-winning landscape architect Professor Martin Hallinan, the garden is named after the patron saint of gardeners and is a tranquil space planted with native Irish species.

Guided tours of the **Irish National Stud** last around 45 minutes. From February to May, it's possible to see tiny future champions in the foaling unit. In the paddock, you can catch a glimpse of well-known legends that have won prestigious races such as the Cheltenham Gold Cup, Champion Hurdle, and the Royal Ascot Gold Cup.

Meanwhile, the **Irish Racehorse Experience** provides visitors with an insight into the world of horse racing. The interactive experience includes a look at renowned trainer Jessica Harrington's yard and the chance to 'train' a racehorse, choose your colours, and prepare it for the racetrack.

Winter visitors should note, the Irish National Stud & Gardens closes from late December to early February.

GETTING THERE

Approximate time and distance from Dublin: one hour (58km/36 miles).
Driving: From the M7 take exit 13 in the direction of Nurney on the R415 as far as Newtown Cross. Turn left and continue to the T-Junction. Follow signage for Irish National Stud & Gardens.

DAYTRIP: KILKENNY

Renowned for its ruby-red Smithwick's Ale, its hurling prowess – Kilkenny is the most successful county team in the history of the sport – and for its Medieval Mile trail, the 'Marble City' offers plenty to enthral daytrippers.

Start your tour of Kilkenny's Medieval Mile at **Kilkenny Castle**. Built in the 12th century, it was the home of the Butler family, who were the earls, marquesses, and dukes of Ormond for nearly 600 years. The castle now welcomes thousands of visitors each year, all eager to discover the story of one of the country's most powerful dynasties. Guided tours take you on a journey through 800 years of the castle's history, giving you the opportunity to stop and admire the splendour of its rooms and beautiful collection of furniture, paintings, tapestries, and objets d'art. The adjacent park and gardens are also open to the public year-round and feature a formal terraced rose garden and woodland walks.

For a more in-depth look at Kilkenny's medieval heritage, call into the nearby **Medieval Mile Museum**, where you can hear stories about the knights, wealthy families, and local characters who have contributed to the city's rich and colourful history.

Not far from here is another marvel – **St Canice's Cathedral and Round Tower**. Recognised as Ireland's best preserved medieval cathedral, it has been a place of worship since the 6th century. Climb the cathedral's round tower to see the city from a whole new perspective.

Just a short walk from the cathedral is Smithwick's brewery. Founded by John Smithwick in 1710 on the site of a Franciscan abbey, it continued brewing from the same location until 2013, when its operations moved to Dublin. Today, the **Smithwick's Experience** welcomes visitors to explore the original brewery during a one-hour interactive guided tour which also includes a complimentary pint of Smithwick's Ale.

More craic agus ceol (Irish for 'fun and music') is to be found at the **Hole in the Wall**, a cosy tavern-style bar and music venue housed in Archer Inner House, the oldest surviving townhouse in Ireland which dates back to 1582.

GETTING THERE

Approximate time and distance from Dublin: one hour and 23 minutes (129km/80 miles).

By bus: Bus Éireann (buseireann.ie) provides a Dublin to Kilkenny service. Buses depart from Busáras bus station on Store Street. Journey time is approximately one hour and 40 minutes.

By train: The train journey between Dublin and Kilkenny is around one hour and 38 minutes. Operated by Irish Rail (irishrail.ie), the service departs from Dublin Heuston and arrives in Kilkenny MacDonagh.

Driving: Head north-east on the M50 toll road. At junction 9, exit onto the N7 towards Limerick/Cork/Waterford/N8/N9. Continue on the N7 before heading onto the M7 and when you reach the M9, follow signs for N10 Waterford/Kilkenny/Kilcullen. At junction 8, take the N10 exit to Kilkenny.

THE ESSENTIALS

Hit the ground running with these useful tips about Dublin's transport system, local culture, and other idiosyncrasies.

DUBLIN WEATHER

Ireland has a temperate climate with warm summers and generally mild winters. Year-round temperatures usually vary between 3°C to 19°C and rarely below -1°C or above 22°C.

The weather can be unpredictable, however – and quite often, it's a four-seasons-in-one-day kind of situation. When packing for your trip to Dublin, consider taking clothes that can be layered – a light rain jacket is also handy to have, no matter what time of year you visit.

FESTIVALS AND EVENTS IN DUBLIN

The world-famous St Patrick's Festival parade takes place annually on 17 March, with a cast of over 4000 performers, musicians, dancers and artists, as well as smaller satellite events around the city during the week of the festival.

Every year, special celebrations take place across Dublin city and in the coastal village of Sandycove to mark Bloomsday on 16 June – the date on which James Joyce's novel *Ulysses* is set. Expect to see Edwardian-dressed Joyce devotees partaking in themed breakfasts, literary readings and other activities.

Outdoor concerts and festivals featuring major international artists take place at venues across the city over the summer months, including College Green, Iveagh Gardens, Royal Hospital Kilmainham, Phoenix Park, Aviva Stadium, and Croke Park.

For one Friday night in September each year, Culture Night sees museums, galleries, theatres and other venues offering free late-night events. Visit culturenight.ie for more information.

Dublin's New Year's Festival is a two-day event featuring a ticketed countdown concert at North Wall Quay on 31 December and a range of celebrations in Temple Bar on New Year's Day.

PUBLIC HOLIDAYS

There are ten official public holidays in Ireland: 1 January (New Year's Day), first Monday in February or when 1 February falls on a Friday (St Brigid's Day), St Patrick's Day (17 March), Easter Monday, first Monday in May (May Bank Holiday), first Monday in June (June Bank Holiday), first Monday in August (August Bank Holiday), last Monday in October (October Bank Holiday), 25 December (Christmas Day), and

26 December (St Stephen's Day). Banks, schools and most offices and small businesses close on these dates, but larger shops, retailers and cultural attractions are usually open. Public transport also usually operates, but on a reduced schedule. There is no public transport on Christmas Day.

IRISH LANGUAGE

Although Irish (Gaeilge) is one of the two official languages of Ireland and is taught as part of the Irish school curriculum, Irish is generally not spoken by Dubliners on a day-to-day basis. However, if you're taking public transport in Dublin, you'll hear the stops being announced in both Irish and English. The same goes for street signs and road signs around the capital – place names always appear in both languages.

A BIT OF CRAIC

In Dublin, we often have our own way of speaking English – slang terms and turns of phrase that are worth knowing to save any potential confusion …

Grand: Contrary to what you might think, this is not used to express that something is amazing or exceedingly good, but rather that it's fine, average or just okay. 'How was the film last night?' 'Ah, it was grand – nothing great, like.'

Thanks a million: An emphatic 'thank you'. 'Here, you nearly left your phone in the taxi.' 'Ah, thanks a million.'

Penneys: The world's first Primark store – located on Mary Street – and we also joke that it's the 'Irish for thank you' if someone compliments your attire. 'I love your dress.' 'Penneys.'

Fair play: Used to congratulate someone or say well done. 'Fair play on the new house.' Or, 'Fair play to him, he passed his driving test first time.'

Gas: This has nothing to do with the elements of the periodic table. 'Gas' means funny or amusing. 'Sarah's cat is able to open the front door – he's gas.' Or you might use it to show disbelief about something funny that happened: 'No way – that's gas.'

Craic: Pronounced 'crack', this generally means 'good fun'. 'It was good craic in the pub last night – you should have been there.' But it's also another way of saying, 'What's up with so and so?' For example, 'What's the craic with the heating in here? It's freezing.' You might also use it as a friendly greeting: 'Ah Eoin, what's the craic? I haven't seen you in ages.'

THE ESSENTIALS

Lashing: Means pouring rain. 'Don't go yet – wait 'til it stops lashing.' Or, 'It's lashing rain out.'

What's the story? (also, Story?): Similar to 'What's the craic?' – used to greet someone. 'Tara, what's the story? How are you getting on with the new job?'

Deadly: A way to say you're impressed by something. 'Their new album is actually deadly. Have you heard it yet?' Or, 'I'm going to that new place in Stoneybatter later.' 'Deadly. Let me know what it's like.'

Yer man or Yer wan: Used when you don't know the name of a man or woman – or when something about them displeases you. 'Look at yer man over there in the shorts, does he think it's summer?' Or, 'Ask yer wan at the till, she'll tell you what time the shop closes at.'

Scoops: Means a few pints or drinks. 'We're going for a few scoops later in town.'

GETTING TO/FROM DUBLIN

If arriving by plane, the city centre is approximately 15km from Dublin Airport.

Bus: Dublin Bus operates from the Dublin Airport Bus Park in Zone 15. Routes 16 and 41 service Dublin city centre. The most frequent airport service is the Airlink Express. The Airlink 747 route serves mostly the northside of Dublin city and departs every ten minutes during peak times, while the 757 route serves mostly the southside of the city and departs every 30 minutes from the city centre and from Dublin Airport.

The Leap Visitor Card: The Leap Visitor Card is the most cost-effective public transport card for tourists and visitors planning to travel around Dublin. It offers unlimited travel over your selected time period on Dublin city bus services (operated by Dublin Bus and Go-Ahead Ireland), Luas, DART and Commuter Rail. Leap Visitor Cards are available to buy online and from participating retailers in Dublin. In Dublin Airport, the card can be purchased from Spar (T2 Arrivals) or WHSmith (T1 Arrivals). Prices vary depending on the option you choose: 1 day (24 hours) – €8, 3 days (72 hours) – €16, 7 days (168 hours) – €32.

Aircoach: Aircoach covers routes to both Dublin city centre and county and departs from just outside Terminal 1, Zone 2, and Terminal 2, Zone 20. Check online for the latest Aircoach information and to book your ticket.

The Essentials

THE ESSENTIALS

Dublin Express: Dublin Express offers premium-quality coach transfers between Dublin Airport and numerous stops throughout the city centre including Temple Bar, Trinity College, O'Connell Street and Heuston railway station. Coaches depart outside Terminals 1 and 2. Onboard services include free customer Wi-Fi, USB charging points and toilet facilities. Tickets should be pre-booked online to ensure availability.

Taxi: Follow taxi signage from Terminal 1 and Terminal 2 to the taxi ranks outside Terminal 1 and Terminal 2. The journey to Dublin city centre takes 25–45 minutes depending on traffic and costs around €30–€40.

FREE NOW: Using the FREE NOW taxi app, you can arrange to be picked up from Zone 18. When you select Dublin Airport as your pick-up point address, you will receive instructions on how to get there.

GETTING AROUND DUBLIN

Walk: Walking is by far the easiest way to get around central Dublin. The city centre's compact size means it's often much quicker to get to your destination by foot than if you were to wait for a bus or Luas to connect you to your destination.

NOW dublinbikes: NOW dublinbikes is a bike rental scheme that operates across the city centre. To rent a bike, you need to first sign up to the NOW dublinbikes app. Choose the location of your choice and select 'release a bike'. The first 30 minutes of each journey are free; after that a small fee applies – for example, a three-hour rental costs €3.50.

Dublin Bus: Dublin Bus offers the most comprehensive route network when travelling to/from areas or neighbourhoods north or south of the Liffey. Tip: When waiting at a stop, it's important that you signal to the driver that you want them to stop for you; otherwise, they will pass you by. Extend your arm in front of you, as if you're hailing a cab.

It's nice to be nice: Something else that sometimes surprises visitors is that Dubliners generally thank the bus driver as they exit the bus.

Luas: Luas (which means 'speed' in Irish) is Dublin's light rail transit system (tram) and operates two lines – Luas Red Line and Luas Green Line. You can switch between the two lines at Abbey Street, O'Connell – GPO, and Marlborough Street.

DART: Dublin Area Rapid Transit (DART) is the easiest way to get to coastal villages and towns on the northside or southside of Dublin.

The Essentials

Taxi: Taxis can be hailed in the street and there are designated ranks also located throughout the city centre. All taxis are metred.

FREE NOW: Taxis can be booked quickly and easily through the FREE NOW app.

POSTCODES

Dublin city is divided into 25 postcodes: D1–D18, D20, D22, D24, D6W, North County Dublin, South County Dublin, and West County Dublin. The Liffey slices the county into north and south, with even-numbered postcodes south of the river and odd-numbered postcodes to the north – apart from Dublin 8 and Dublin 20 which encompass areas both north and south of the Liffey.

SHOPPING

City centre retailers generally open 9am–6pm Monday–Saturday, but some shopping centres and larger department stores open later, until 8pm or 9pm. In the weeks before Christmas, many retailers extend their opening hours. On Sundays, most city centre stores open from 12–6pm.

Supermarkets: Don't forget your reusable shopping bag. A plastic bag levy of 22 cent per shopping bag currently applies.

Tax-free shopping for non-EU travellers: Visitors to Ireland from outside the European Union (EU), including England, Scotland and Wales, can avail of tax-free shopping in Ireland when they spend over €75. This also includes Irish nationals living permanently in Great Britain or non-EU countries. Residents from Northern Ireland are not eligible. To claim a tax refund, non-EU shoppers can request and complete a tax-free form from participating shops or department stores when making their purchase. Your passport or flight details may be required as proof of residency. To simplify refunds, payment should be made by credit card. On departure from Dublin Airport, non-EU passengers should return the completed form to one of the numerous Planet Payment kiosks in the airport. All tax refunds are subject to customs approval.

PUBS AND NIGHTLIFE

As of 2023, late licensed pubs can serve until 1.30am on weekends and nightclubs until 2.30am.

Pubs open from 10.30am–12.30am seven days a week. Late bars with special licences open until 2.30am and some nightclubs remain open until 6am.

The legal drinking age in Ireland is 18, but you'll find some pubs, clubs and late bars have an over-21s policy – ID may be requested to gain admission.

PHOTO CREDITS

THANK YOU

(Go raibh maith agat)

---

*Thank you to the amazing team at Hardie Grant Explore –
Melissa Kayser, Megan Cuthbert, and Amanda Louey – for
persevering with* Beyond the Cobblestones in Dublin *over
the past number of years, despite challenging circumstances –
not least, a global pandemic. Thanks also to the brilliant
Meg Walker for helping to make the editing process run
so smoothly.*

*To the shopkeepers, bakers, baristas, creatives, and bold
visionaries featured in these pages – thank you for bringing a
little extra joy to neighbourhoods all around Dublin.*

*Thank you to Joe Ladrigan for capturing Dublin in
such an interesting, unique way, and to the typesetter Hannah
Schubert and the Muse Muse team who have contributed to
the beautiful look and feel of this book, as well as Catherine
Turner for your thoughtful and thorough proofreading.*

*A special thank you also to my family for your insights
and encouragement, especially my parents – thank you for
sharing your stories about Dublin.*

Fiona Hilliard is a travel writer and digital content creator from Dublin,
Ireland. She has contributed to leading travel publications including
Forbes Travel and has also managed travel content for Europe's largest
airline. Fiona's travel writing career took off after studying languages and
journalism at university. Her adventures have taken her far and wide, from
exploring the vibrant markets of Oaxaca, Mexico to camping under the stars
in Jordan's Wadi Rum desert, but she is never happier than when she is
uncovering hidden gems in her native city.

Published in 2023 by Hardie Grant Explore,
an imprint of Hardie Grant Publishing

Hardie Grant Explore (Melbourne)
Wurundjeri Country
Building 1, 658 Church Street
Richmond, Victoria 3121

Hardie Grant Explore (Sydney)
Gadigal Country
Level 7, 45 Jones Street
Ultimo, NSW 2007

www.hardiegrant.com/au/explore

The maps in this publication incorporate data from
OpenStreetMap www.openstreetmap.org/copyright

OpenStreetMap is open data, licensed under the
Open Data Commons Open Database License
(ODbL) by the OpenStreetMap Foundation (OSMF).

https://opendatacommons.org/licenses/odbl/1-0/

Any rights in individual contents of the database are
licensed under the Database Contents License:
https://opendatacommons.org/licenses/dbcl/1-0/

Data extracts via Geofabrik GmbH
https://www.geofabrik.de

A catalogue record for this
book is available from the
National Library of Australia

Hardie Grant acknowledges the Traditional Owners
of the Country on which we work, the Wurundjeri
People of the Kulin Nation and the Gadigal People
of the Eora Nation, and recognises their continuing
connection to the land, waters and culture. We pay
our respects to their Elders past and present.

Beyond the Cobblestones in Dublin
ISBN 9781741176940

10 9 8 7 6 5 4 3 2 1

Project editor Amanda Louey
Editor Meg Walker
Proofreader Catherine Turner
Cartographer Claire Johnston
Design Muse Muse
Typesetting Hannah Schubert

Colour reproduction by Hannah Schubert and
Splitting Image Colour Studio

Printed and bound in China by
LEO Paper Products LTD.

FSC
www.fsc.org
MIX
Paper from
responsible sources
FSC® C020056

The paper this book is printed
on is certified against the
Forest Stewardship Council®
Standards and other sources.
FSC® promotes environmentally
responsible, socially beneficial
and economically viable
management of the world's
forests.